Instructions on page 49.

ROMANTIC COTTON GALLERY

a

b

c

d

e

f

Fabrics used to make pieces are shown in actula size.

g

Fabrics used to make pieces are shown in actual size.

a

b

c

d

e

Intructions for Framed Picture on page 52, and for Wall Hanging on page 53.

Instructions on page 54.

Fabrics used to make pieces are shown in actual size.

a

b

c

d

e

f

g

h

i

5

Instructions on page 58.

Same pattern on varied fabrics
(Reduced to 1/4 size).

Fabrics used to make
pieces are shown
in actual size.

			a	
		b	c	
	d	e	f	
g	h	i	j	
k	l	m	n	o

| p | q | r | s | t | u | v |

Brighten Up Your Room

with Colorful Patchwork

Instructions on page 57.

Same pattern on varied fabrics.

10

Instructions on page 59.

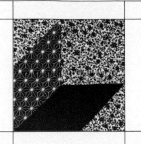

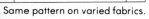

Same pattern on varied fabrics.

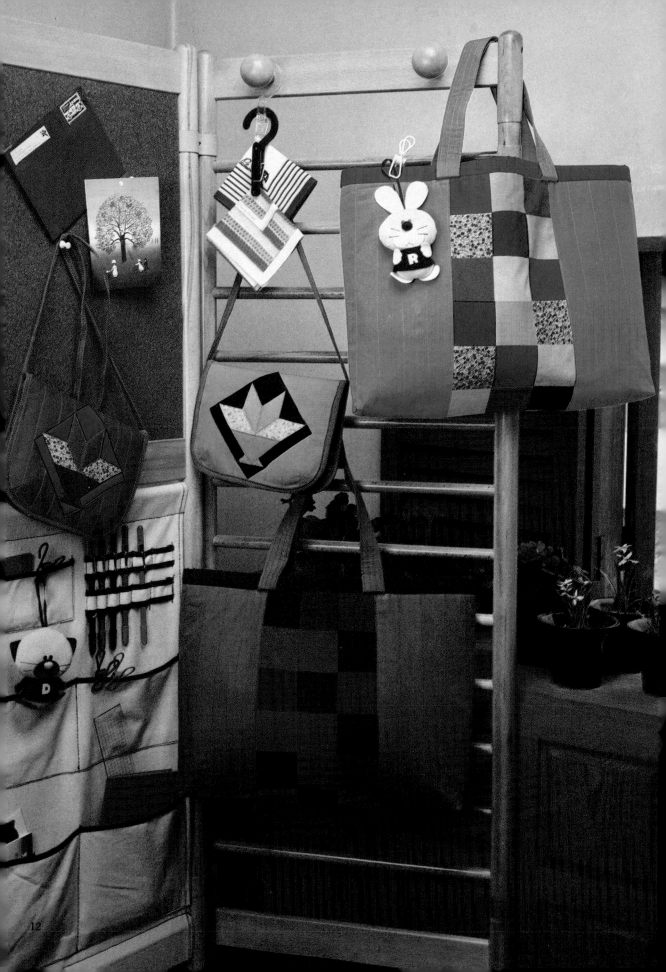

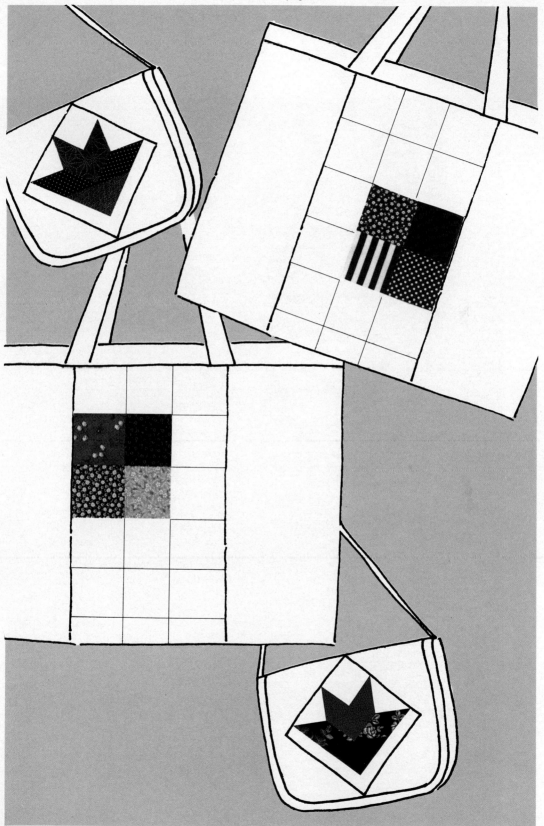

Same pattern on varied fabrics.

LOVELY COTTON

HOUSE

Instructions on page 63.

Same pattern on varied fabrics.

Fabrics used to make pieces are shown in actual size.

Same pattern on varied fabrics

Instructions on page 64.

Instructions on page 65.

Instructions on page 68.

KEEP COOL

Instructions on page 88.

AT SUMMER

Fabrics used to make
pieces are shown
in actual size.

a   b   c

a   b   c

a   b   c

Instructions for Pillows at left on page 67, and for Pillows at right on page 69.

24

Same pattern on varied fabrics.

Instructions for Shoo-fly Apron at left on page 70,
Pinwheel Apron at right on page 76, and Navy and White Apron on page 74.

c

a

b

Fabrics used to make pieces are shown in actual size.

a

b

c

d

e

f

g

Instructions on page 73.

28

h

j

k

i

Same pattern on varied fabrics.

s

r

q

p

l

m

n

o

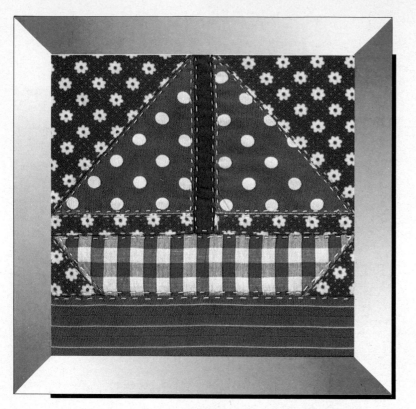

YACHT

SCHOOL

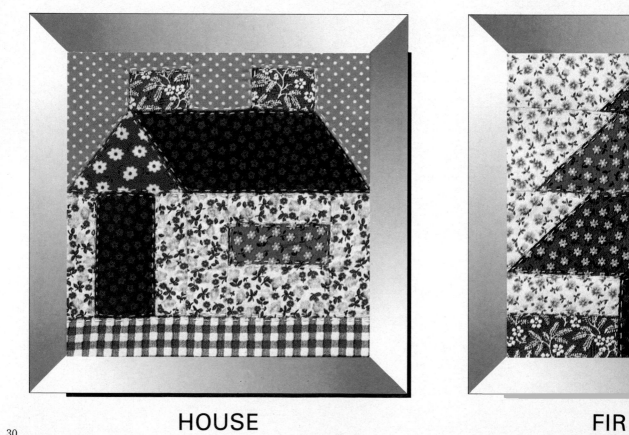

HOUSE

FIR

30

HOUSE

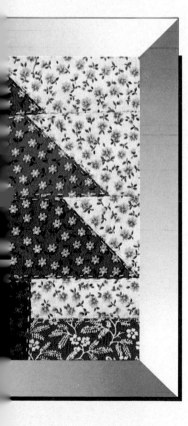

TULIP

Instructions on page 71.

FOR SUMMER LIFE

Fabrics used to make a piece is shown in actual size.

Instructions on page 78.

Fabrics for red blocks. **a**

b

c

d

d

Fabrics for brown blocks.

c

a

b

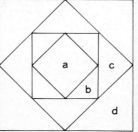

Instructions on page 79.

Same pattern on varied fabrics (Reduced to 1/6 size).

Fabrics used to make pieces are
shown in actual size.

a   a

b

c   c

Fabrics for pink pillow. →

← Fabrics for
green pillow.

PLAY WITH BLOCKS.....

MODERN PATCHWORK

Instructions on page 82.

Fabrics for blue bag. → a   b

Fabrics used to make
pieces are shown in
actual size.

40

Fabrics for → c   d   e
red purse.

Fabrics for green bag. → a   b

Instructions for Tote Bags on page 86,
and for Striped Purses on page 87.

Fabrics for green purse. → c   d   e

41

a   b   Fabrics used to make pieces are shown
in actual size.

Instructions on page 90.
(Use same pattern on varied fabrics for Framed Picture.)

c   d   e   f

Instructions on page 98.
(Use same pattern on varied fabrics for Framed Picture.)

43

Instructions on page 90.

Fabrics used to make pieces are shown in actual size.

a   b   c   d   e

← Fabrics for blue placemat.

Fabrics for red placemat. ↑

48

INSTRUCTIONS TO COMPLETE THE PREVIOUS PAGES

FRAMED PATCHWORK PICTURES, shown on page 1

For Top Picture: MATERIALS: Cotton fabrics (See the photo for colors and designs.): 18cm by 8cm each for (a) (b) and (c); 22cm by 8cm for (d); 20cm by 14cm for (e); 34cm by 16cm for (f); 25cm square for lining. #50 white cotton sewing thread. Quilt batting, 25cm square. Frame, 23.3cm square (inside measurement).
FINISHED SIZE: 23.3cm square
DIRECTIONS:
1. Cut out pieces, adding 0.7cm seam allowance all around.

2. Following the diagram for placement, sew pieces together in alphabetical order shown on page 62, using method A on page 102.
3. Place batting between pieced picture and lining and quilt along quilting lines shown in the diagram.
4. Trim off excess 0.7cm from the finished line and overcast edges.

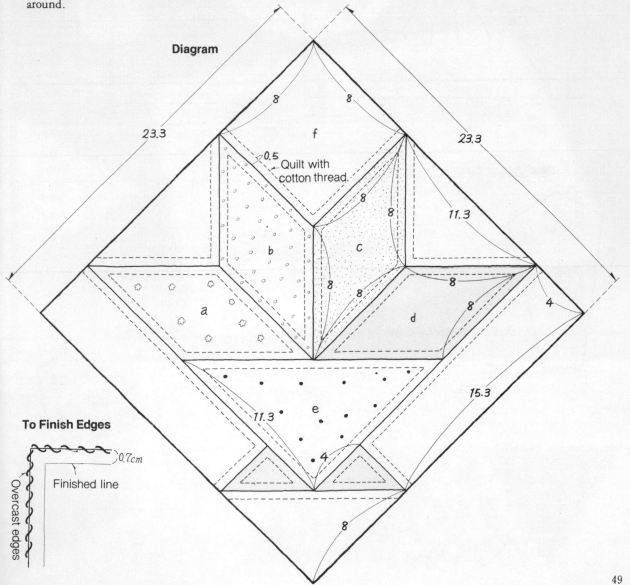

49

DRESDEN PLATE PICTURE (bottom left):
MATERIALS: Cotton fabrics (See the list below.): 27cm square for lining. Light olive green cotton sewing thread. Quilt batting, 27cm square. Frame, 22.5cm square (inside measurement).
FINISHED SIZE: 22.5cm square

Diagram

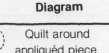
Quilt around appliquéd piece.

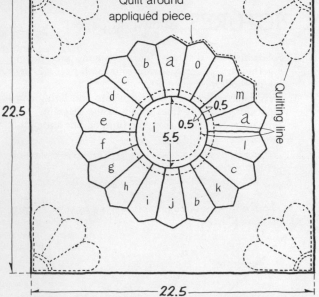

22.5

22.5

Quilting line

0.5
0.5
5.5
a

Designs and Required Amounts of Fabrics

	Color and designs	Required pieces	Required amounts
a	Unbleached fabric with flowers	2	9cm X 6.5cm
b	Yellow with flowers	"	"
c	White with black print	"	"
d	Light green	1	4.5 × 6.5
e	Dark red with flowers	"	"
f	Blue with brown print	"	"
g	Dark brown with flowers	"	"
h	Beige with brown checks	"	"
i	Cream with white dots	1 each	11.5 × 7
j	Light pink with flowers	1	4.5 × 6.5
k	Brown with flowers	"	"
l	Red with white dots	"	"
m	Olive green	"	"
n	Cobalt blue with flowers	"	"
o	Black with flowers	"	"
Background fabric	Light olive green	"	27cm square

Patch Pattern (Actual Size)

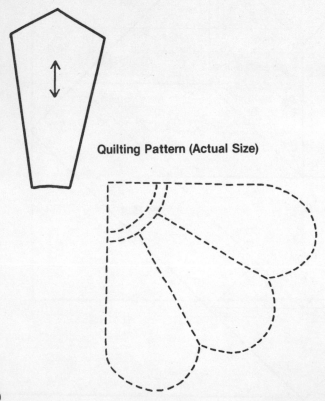

Quilting Pattern (Actual Size)

Directions
1. Cut out pieces, adding 0.7cm seam allowance all around.
2. With right sides together, stitch along dash line. Turn seam to one side and crease 0.1cm from seam.
   (Continue to sew pieces together to make a circle.)

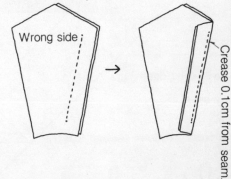

Wrong side

Crease 0.1cm from seam.

3. Turn 0.7cm seam allowance to wrong side and press. Fold all seam allowances of (A) in same manner.

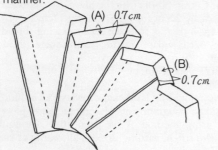

(A) 0.7cm

(B)
0.7cm

Then fold all seam allowances of (B) in same manner.

4. Center pieced circle on background. Appliqué circle to background in tiny slip stitches.

5. Place appliquéd piece, quilt batting and lining together and quilt as shown in the diagram.

Slip-stitch center piece with tiny stitches, turning in seam allowance as you sew.

STAR PICTURE (bottom right)
MATERIALS: Cotton fabrics (See the photo for colors and designs.): 33cm by 15cm for (f); 30cm by 13cm for (g); 22cm square for lining. #25 six-strand embroidery floss in dark red. #50 white cotton sewing thread. Quilt batting, 22cm square. Frame, 20cm square (inside measurement).
FINISHED SIZE: 20cm square
DIRECTIONS:
1. Cut out pieces, adding 0.7cm seam allowance all around.

2. Following the diagram for placement, sew pieces together, using method A on page 102. Embroider on center piece.
3. Place batting between pieced picture and lining and quilt as shown in the diagram.
4. Trim off excess of edges and overcast in same manner as Plate Picture.

To Make Up
Join in sequences (A)-(E).

Embroidery Pattern (Actual Size)

Diagram

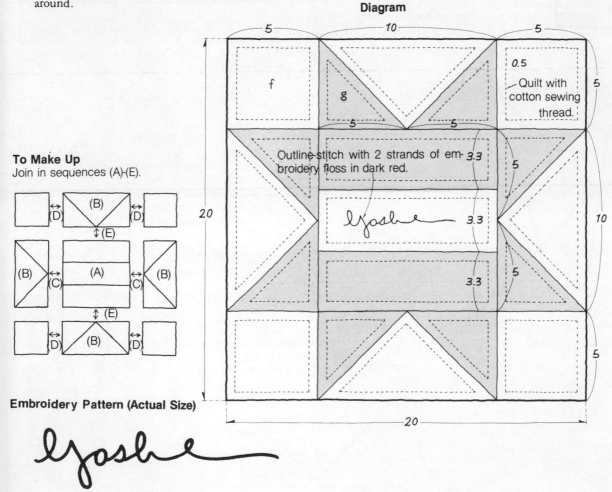

FLOWER BASKET PICTURE, shown on page 2

Appliqué Pattern (Actual Size)

MATERIALS: Cotton fabrics (See the photo for colors and designs.): 72cm by 22cm for (a); 73cm by 11cm for (b); 32cm square for lining. #50 black cotton sewing thread. Quilt batting, 32cm square. Frame, 30cm square (inside measurement).

FINISHED SIZE: 30cm square

DIRECTIONS:

1. Cut out pieces, adding 1cm seam allowance all around.
2. Following the diagram for placement, sew pieces together, using method A on page 102. Appliqué handle in slip stitch, turning in seam allowance as you sew.
3. Place batting between pieced picture and lining and quilt as shown in the diagram.

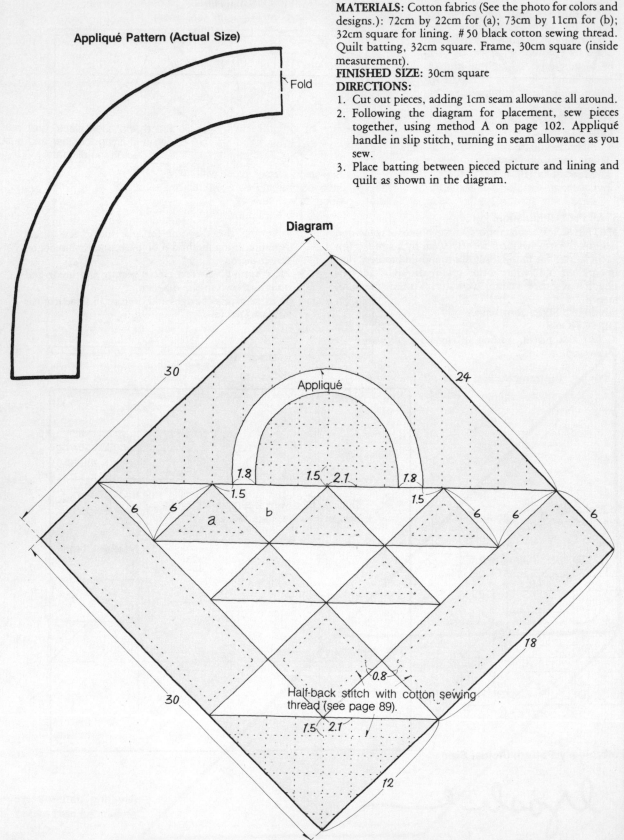

Fold

Diagram

FLYING SWALLOWS WALL HANGING, shown on page 3

MATERIALS: Cotton fabrics (See the photo for colors and designs.): 84cm by 26cm for (c); 83cm by 73cm for (d); 60cm by 39cm for (e); 66cm by 14cm of olive green. Silk sewing thread. Heavy-duty silk sewing thread in white, brown and dark brown. Quilt batting, 63cm square.

FINISHED SIZE: 63.5cm square

DIRECTIONS:

1. Make templates for patches. Cut out pieces, adding seam allowance all around.
2. Following the diagram for placement, sew pieces together using method A on page 102.
3. Place pieced top, batting and lining together. Quilt along quilting lines shown in the diagram, using indicated thread.
4. Bind the edge of each side with olive green strip and then bind top and bottom edges in same manner.

Diagram
(Add 0.7cm seam allowance)

Bind the edge.

Quilting lines

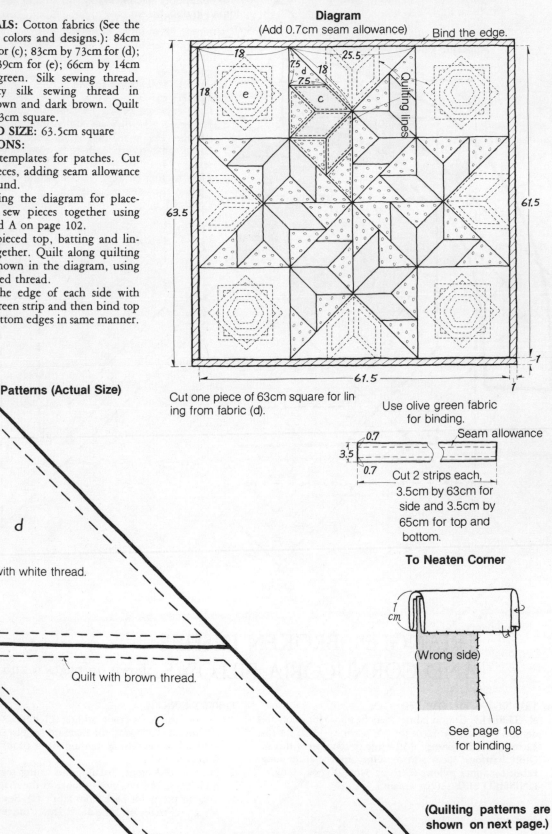

Cut one piece of 63cm square for lining from fabric (d).

Patterns (Actual Size)

d

Quilt with white thread.

Quilt with brown thread.

c

Use olive green fabric for binding.

Seam allowance

Cut 2 strips each, 3.5cm by 63cm for side and 3.5cm by 65cm for top and bottom.

To Neaten Corner

(Wrong side)

See page 108 for binding.

(Quilting patterns are shown on next page.)

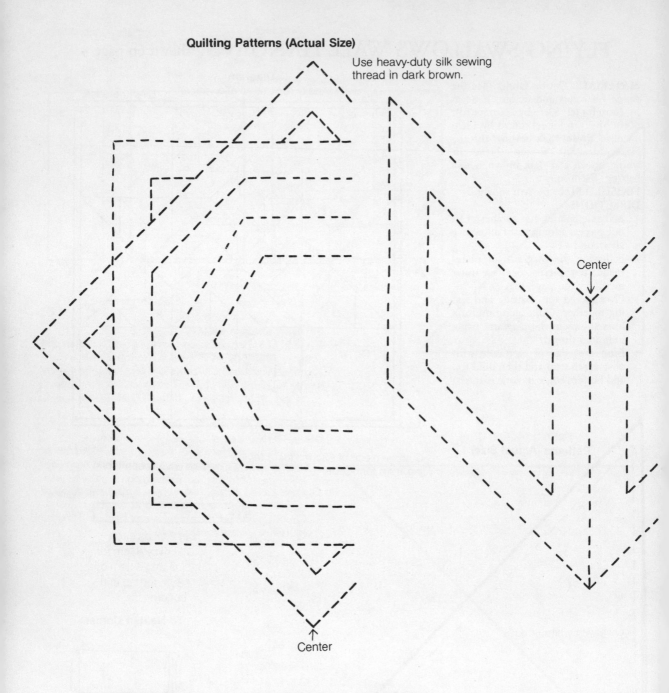

Use heavy-duty silk sewing thread in dark brown.

Center

Center

TRIANGLES, BROKEN DISHES
AND CORNUCOPIA PILLOWS, shown on pages 4 and 5

TRIANGLES PILLOW, left
MATERIALS: Cotton fabrics (See the photo for colors and designs.): 80cm by 32cm for (a); 60cm by 17cm for (b); 32cm square for lining. #50 white cotton sewing thread. Quilt batting, 32cm square. One zipper, 26cm long. Fabric for inner pillow, 66cm by 34cm. Kapok, 170g.
FINISHED SIZE: 30cm square

DIRECTIONS:
1. Cut out pieces for Front, adding 0.7cm seam allowance all around. Following the diagram for placement, sew pieces together, using method B on page 104. Turn seams to (b) side.
2. Place pieced Front, batting and lining together and quilt along quilting lines shown in the diagram.
3. Cut out pieces for Back from fabric (a). Sew zipper in place and make up for pillow. Insert inner pillow.

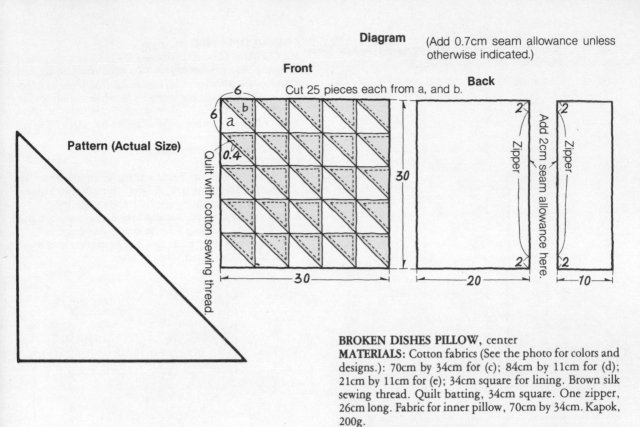

Diagram (Add 0.7cm seam allowance unless otherwise indicated.)

Pattern (Actual Size)

Front
Cut 25 pieces each from a, and b.

Back

6
6
b
a
0.4
Quilt with cotton sewing thread.
30
30
2
2
2
2
Zipper
Zipper
Add 2cm seam allowance here.
20
10

BROKEN DISHES PILLOW, center
MATERIALS: Cotton fabrics (See the photo for colors and designs.): 70cm by 34cm for (c); 84cm by 11cm for (d); 21cm by 11cm for (e); 34cm square for lining. Brown silk sewing thread. Quilt batting, 34cm square. One zipper, 26cm long. Fabric for inner pillow, 70cm by 34cm. Kapok, 200g.
FINISHED SIZE: 32cm square
DIRECTIONS:
1. Cut out pieces for Front, adding seam allowance all around. Sew pieces together, using method A on page 102.
2. Place pieced Front, batting and lining together and quilt along quilting lines shown in the diagram.
3. Cut out pieces for Back. Sew zipper in place. Make up for pillow. Insert inner pillow.

Pattern (Actual Size)

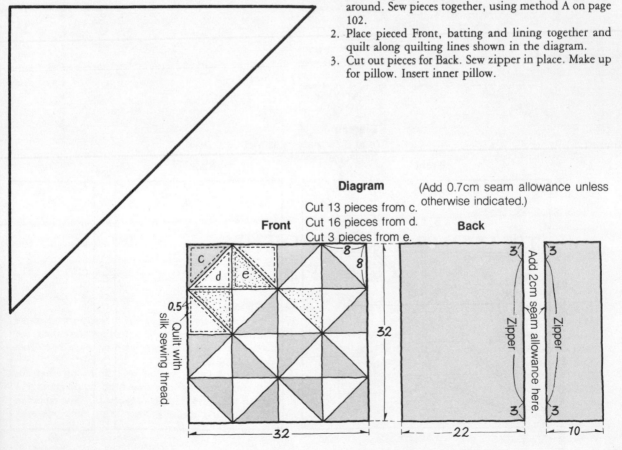

Diagram (Add 0.7cm seam allowance unless otherwise indicated.)
Cut 13 pieces from c.
Cut 16 pieces from d.
Cut 3 pieces from e.

Front

Back

c
d
e
8
8
0.5
Quilt with silk sewing thread.
32
32
3
3
3
3
Zipper
Zipper
Add 2cm seam allowance here.
22
10

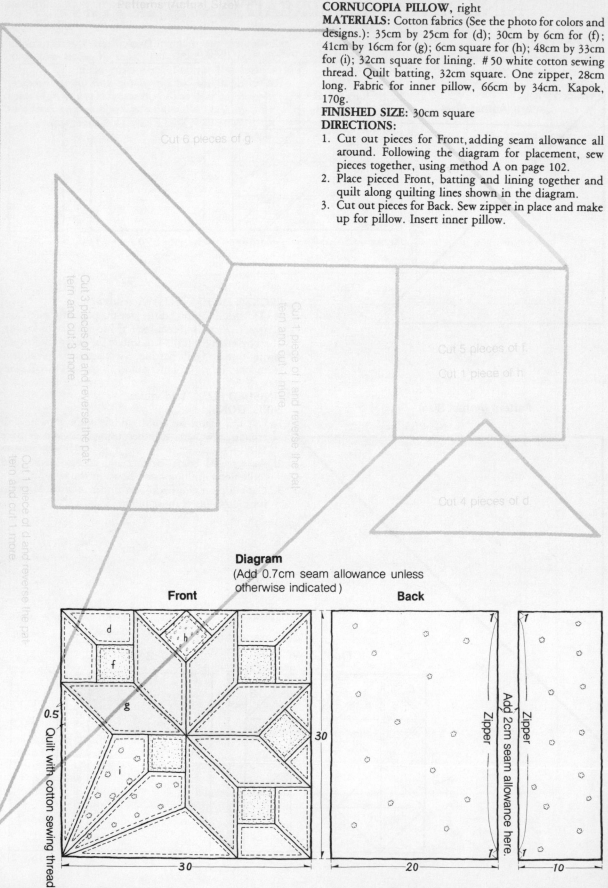

Patterns (Actual Size)

Cut 6 pieces of g.

Cut 3 pieces of d and reverse the pattern and cut 3 more.

Cut 1 piece of i and reverse the pattern and cut 1 more.

Cut 1 piece of d and reverse the pattern and cut 1 more.

Cut 5 pieces of f.

Cut 1 piece of h

Cut 4 pieces of d

CORNUCOPIA PILLOW, right

MATERIALS: Cotton fabrics (See the photo for colors and designs.): 35cm by 25cm for (d); 30cm by 6cm for (f); 41cm by 16cm for (g); 6cm square for (h); 48cm by 33cm for (i); 32cm square for lining. #50 white cotton sewing thread. Quilt batting, 32cm square. One zipper, 28cm long. Fabric for inner pillow, 66cm by 34cm. Kapok, 170g.

FINISHED SIZE: 30cm square

DIRECTIONS:

1. Cut out pieces for Front, adding seam allowance all around. Following the diagram for placement, sew pieces together, using method A on page 102.
2. Place pieced Front, batting and lining together and quilt along quilting lines shown in the diagram.
3. Cut out pieces for Back. Sew zipper in place and make up for pillow. Insert inner pillow.

Diagram
(Add 0.7cm seam allowance unless otherwise indicated)

Front

d
h
f
g
0.5
i

Quilt with cotton sewing thread.

30

30

Back

Zipper

Add 2cm seam allowance here.

Zipper

20

10

NINE-PATCH BEDSPREAD, shown on pages 8 and 9

MATERIALS: Cotton fabrics (See the list below.): sheeting for lining, 90cm by 504cm. Heavy-duty cotton sewing thread in green.

FINISHED SIZE: 250cm by 174cm

DIRECTIONS:

1. Cut out pieces, adding 1cm seam allowance all around. Cut and sew pieces of sheeting to the indicated size (252cm by 176cm).

2. Following the diagram, sew pieces together, using method C on page 105. Start in center and work around and outward. Press seams open.

3. With right sides of pieced top and lining together, stitch three sides with 1cm seams. Turn to right side. Turn in seam allowances of opening and machine-stitch along dash lines shown in the diagram.

Diagram

Front

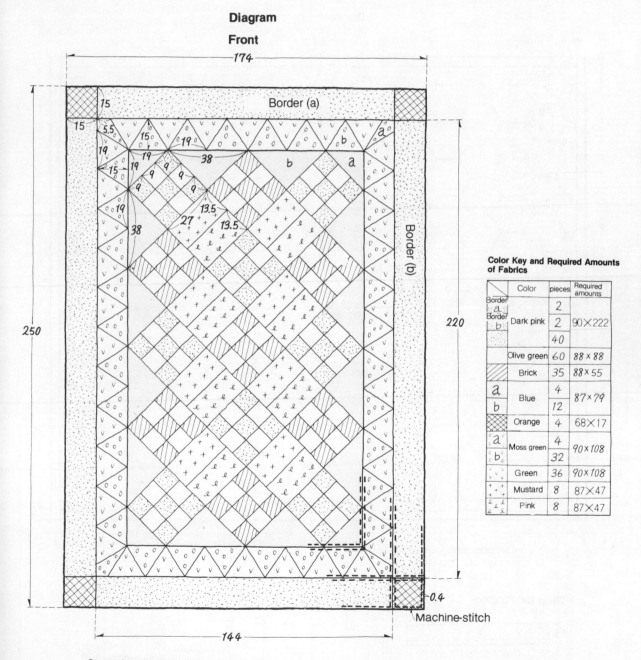

Color Key and Required Amounts of Fabrics

	Color	pieces	Required amounts
Border a / Border b	Dark pink	2 / 2	90×222
		40	
	Olive green	60	88×88
	Brick	35	88×55
a / b	Blue	4 / 12	87×79
	Orange	4	68×17
a / b	Moss green	4 / 32	90×108
	Green	36	90×108
	Mustard	8	87×47
	Pink	8	87×47

Machine-stitch

Sew pieces of sheeting together to make 252cm by 176cm.

GRANDMOTHER'S FLOWER GARDEN TABLE CENTER,

shown on pages 6 and 7

MATERIALS: Cotton fabrics (See the photo for colors and designs.): 90cm square for (a); 35cm by 16cm each for (b) (g) and (i); 18cm by 13cm each for (c) (d) and (e); 30cm by 16cm each for (f) and (s); 4.5cm by 6cm each for (h) and (v); 25cm by 6cm for (j); 18cm by 16cm each for (k) (o) and (q); 7cm by 6cm each for (l) (p) and (r); 45cm by 16cm for (m); 20cm by 6cm for (n); 8cm by 6cm for (t); 21cm by 6cm for(u); 70cm by 14cm of olive green. #50 white cotton sewing thread. Quilt batting, 66.5cm by 57cm.

FINISHED SIZE: 66.8cm by 57.2cm

DIRECTIONS:
1. Cut out pieces, adding seam allowance all around. Following the diagram for placement, sew pieces together, using method A on page 102.
2. Place pieced top, batting and lining together and quilt along seams of each piece.
3. Bind edges of top and bottom with olive green strip. Then bind edges of each side in same manner.

Diagram
(Add 0.7cm seam allowance)

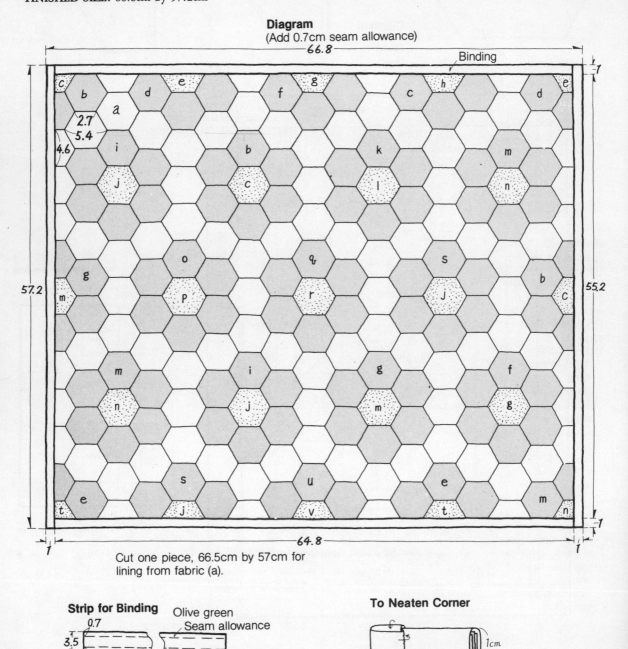

Cut one piece, 66.5cm by 57cm for lining from fabric (a).

Strip for Binding Olive green
Seam allowance
Cut 2 strips each, 3.5cm by 66.8cm for top and bottom, and 3.5cm by 58.6cm for sides.

To Neaten Corner
Wrong side
See page 108 for binding.

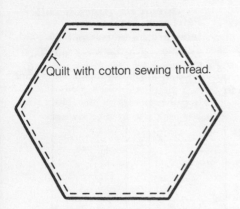

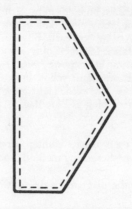

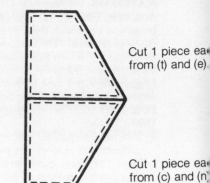

Quilt with cotton sewing thread.

Cut 1 piece each from (t) and (e)

Cut 1 piece each from (c) and (n)

Cut 70 pieces from (a).
Cut 14 pieces from (m).
Cut 12 pieces from (i).
Cut 9 pieces each from (b) (f) (g) and (s).
Cut 6 pieces each from (k) (o) and (q).
Cut 4 pieces each from (c) (d) and (e).
Cut 3 pieces each from (j) and (u).
Cut 1 piece each from (l) (p) and (r).
Cut 2 pieces from (n).

Cut 20 pieces from (a).
Cut 3 pieces each from (b) and (g).
Cut 2 pieces each from (e) and (m).
Cut 1 piece each from (c) (d) (h) (j)(t) and (v).

EIGHT-POINTED STAR PILLOWS, shown on pages 10 and 11

MATERIALS: Fabrics (See the list below.). One zipper, 40cm long. Fabric for inner pillow, 90cm by 46cm. Kapok, 350g.
FINISHED SIZE: 42cm square
DIRECTIONS:
1. Cut out pieces for Front, adding seam allowance all around. Following the diagram for placement, sew pieces together, using method C on page 105. Press seams open.
2. Cut out pieces for Back. Sew zipper in place.
3. With right sides of Front and Back together, stitch all around. Turn to right side. Insert inner pillow.

Diagram
(Add 0.7cm seam allowance unless otherwise indicated)

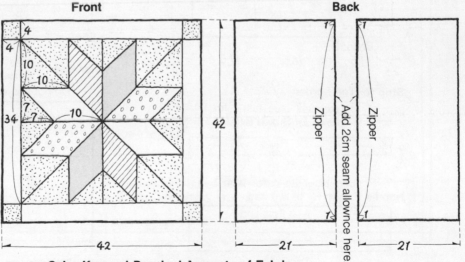

Color Key and Required Amounts of Fabrics

	For pillow at left	For Pillow at right	Required amounts
	Mustard	Brick	17cm × 21cm
	Olive green with wave pattern	Gray	"
	Red	Bright yellow	"
	Beige	Dark yellow	90cm × 15cm
	Dark green	Black	90cm × 44cm
BACK	Dark green	Black	

TOTE BAGS, shown on page 12

MATERIALS: For Blue Bag: Cotton fabrics: blue, 90cm by 92cm; dark blue, 90cm by 12.5cm; light blue, navy blue, dark yellow, beige and beige with floral design, 42cm by 7cm each. Blue cotton sewing thread. Thick non-woven fabric for interlining, 49cm by 72cm. For Brown Bag: Cotton fabrics: light brown, 90cm by 92cm; brown, 90cm by 12.5cm; brick, mustard, yellow brown, bright yellow and dark brown, 42cm by 7cm each. Light brown cotton sewing thread. Same size of interlining as Blue Bag.

FINISHED SIZE: See the diagram.

DIRECTIONS:

1. Cut out 6 patches each from each color, adding seam allowance all around. Sew pieces together, using method C on page 105. Press seams open.
2. Cut out pieces for bag, following the diagram. Make up for bag.

Patchwork Pieces
(Add 0.7cm seam allowance)

Make 2 pieces for Front and Back.

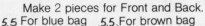
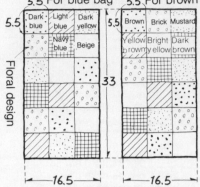

Diagram
(Add 0.7cm seam allowance unless otherwise indicated)

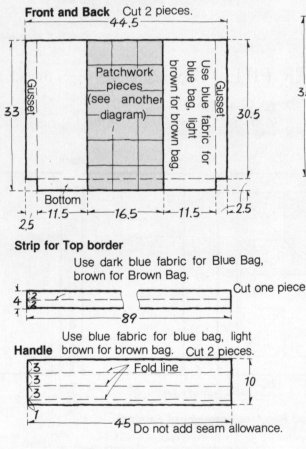

Front and Back Cut 2 pieces.

Patchwork pieces (see another diagram)

Use blue fabric for blue bag, light brown for brown bag.

Interlining Do not add seam allowance here.

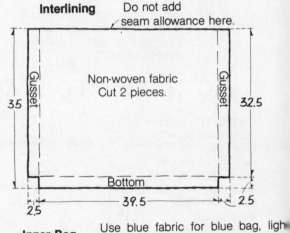

Non-woven fabric Cut 2 pieces.

Strip for Top border

Use dark blue fabric for Blue Bag, brown for Brown Bag.

Cut one piece

Handle Use blue fabric for blue bag, light brown for brown bag. Cut 2 pieces.

Fold line

Interlining for Handle Non-woven fabric cut 2 pieces.

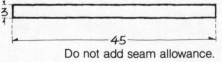

Do not add seam allowance.

Inner Bag Use blue fabric for blue bag, light brown for brown bag. Cut 2 pieces.

Do not add seam allowance here.

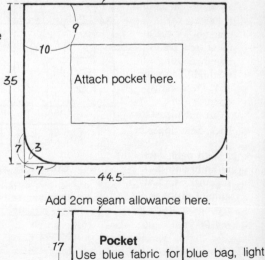

Attach pocket here.

Add 2cm seam allowance here.

Pocket Use blue fabric for blue bag, light brown for brown bag.

Cut 1 piece.

To Make Up

1. Make Front and Back.

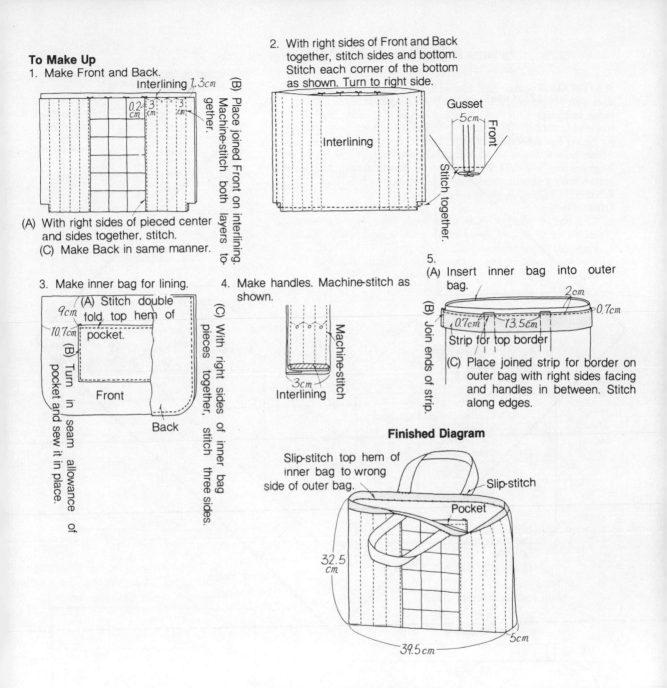

Interlining 1.3cm

(B) Place joined Front on interlining. Machine-stitch both layers together.

(A) With right sides of pieced center and sides together, stitch.
(C) Make Back in same manner.

2. With right sides of Front and Back together, stitch sides and bottom. Stitch each corner of the bottom as shown. Turn to right side.

Interlining

Gusset
5cm
Front
Stitch together.

3. Make inner bag for lining.

9cm
10.7cm
(A) Stitch double fold top hem of pocket.
(B) Turn in seam allowance of pocket and sew it in place.
Front
Back
(C) With right sides of inner bag pieces together, stitch three sides.

4. Make handles. Machine-stitch as shown.

Machine-stitch
3cm
Interlining

5.
(A) Insert inner bag into outer bag.
(B) Join ends of strip.
2cm
0.7cm
0.7cm 13.5cm
Strip for top border
(C) Place joined strip for border on outer bag with right sides facing and handles in between. Stitch along edges.

Finished Diagram

Slip-stitch top hem of inner bag to wrong side of outer bag.
Slip-stitch
Pocket
32.5 cm
39.5 cm
5cm

POCHETTES, shown on page 12

MATERIALS: Cotton fabrics: For Yellow Pochette, left: dark yellow, beige with dark yellow and blue flowers, 44cm by 34cm each; dark blue, 14cm square; brick, 12cm by 6cm. For Gray Pochette: gray, pink with white flowers, 44cm by 34cm each; black, 14cm square; pink, 9cm square. Cotton sewing thread in colors to match fabrics. Thick non-woven fabric for interlining, 50cm by 22cm (for one pochette). Quilt batting, 11cm square (for one). Grosgrain ribbon in light brown for Yellow Pochette, gray for Gray, 1.5cm by 270cm (for one).
FINISHED SIZE: 22cm wide and 17cm deep

DIRECTIONS:
1. Make templates following the diagram. Cut out pieces adding seam allowance all around. Sew pieces together, using method A on page 102.
2. Cut out pieces for Front and Back. Make up for pochette, following instructions on page 63.

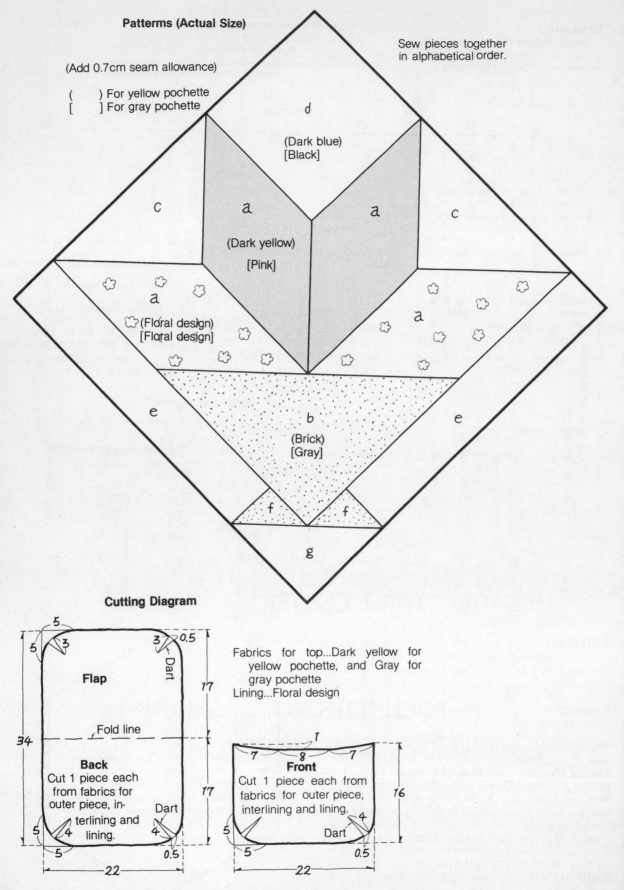

Patterns (Actual Size)

Sew pieces together in alphabetical order.

(Add 0.7cm seam allowance)

(   ) For yellow pochette
[   ] For gray pochette

d
(Dark blue)
[Black]

c

a
(Dark yellow)
[Pink]

a

c

a
(Floral design)
[Floral design]

a

e

b
(Brick)
[Gray]

e

f

f

g

Cutting Diagram

Flap

5

5   3   3   0.5

Dart

17

34   Fold line

Back
Cut 1 piece each from fabrics for outer piece, interlining and lining.

Dart

17

5   4   4
5   0.5

22

Fabrics for top...Dark yellow for yellow pochette, and Gray for gray pochette
Lining...Floral design

1
7   8   7

Front
Cut 1 piece each from fabrics for outer piece, interlining and lining.

16

5   4
Dart
5   0.5

22

62

To Make Up

1. Place fabrics for top, interlining and lining together and quilt as shown with matching thread.

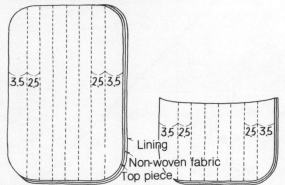

3.5 2.5   2.5 3.5

3.5 2.5   2.5 3.5

Lining
Non-woven fabric
Top piece

2. Sew darts and turn seams to one side.
3. Place quilt batting on wrong side of pieced patches. Turn seam allowance to wrong side.
5. Bind top edges of Front with 23cm long grosgrain ribbon. Place Front on wrong side of Back.

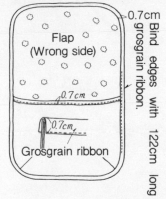

0.7cm

Flap
(Wrong side)

0.7cm

0.7cm

Grosgrain ribbon

Bind edges with 122cm long grosgrain ribbon.

4. Place both layers of 3 on flap. Quilt along quilting lines using matching thread with each piece.

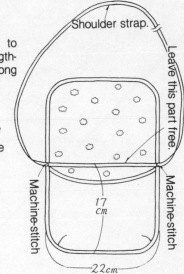

Patched piece

Flap
(Right side)

Quilting

1.5cm

6. Join ends of 125cm ribbon to make circle. Fold in half lengthwise and machine-stitch along edges.

Shoulder strap

1cm

1.5cm

Join to make circle

↓

123cm

7. Sew shoulder strap 6 to wrong side of Back.

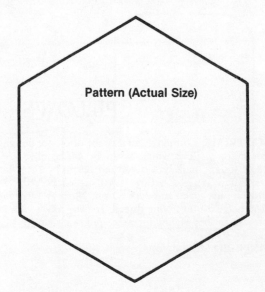

Shoulder strap.

Leave this part free.

Machine-stitch

17 cm

Machine-stitch

22cm

HEXAGON TABLE CENTER, shown on pages 14 and 15

MATERIALS: Sheeting: yellow, 85cm by 30cm; light brown, pink and powder green, 50cm by 16cm each; blue, 46cm by 9cm; unbleached, 62cm square. #50 beige cotton sewing thread. Yellow crochet cotton, 15g. #3 crochet hook.

FINISHED SIZE: See the diagram.

DIRECTIONS:

1. Cut out pieces, adding 0.8cm seam allowance all around. Following the diagram, sew pieces together, using method A on page 102.
2. Place lining on pieced top with wrong sides facing. Slip-stitch lining to wrong side of top, 0.1cm in from the folded edge of top.
3. Stitch along stitching lines of yellow pieces as shown in the diagram.
4. Crochet edging all around.

Pattern (Actual Size)

Diagram

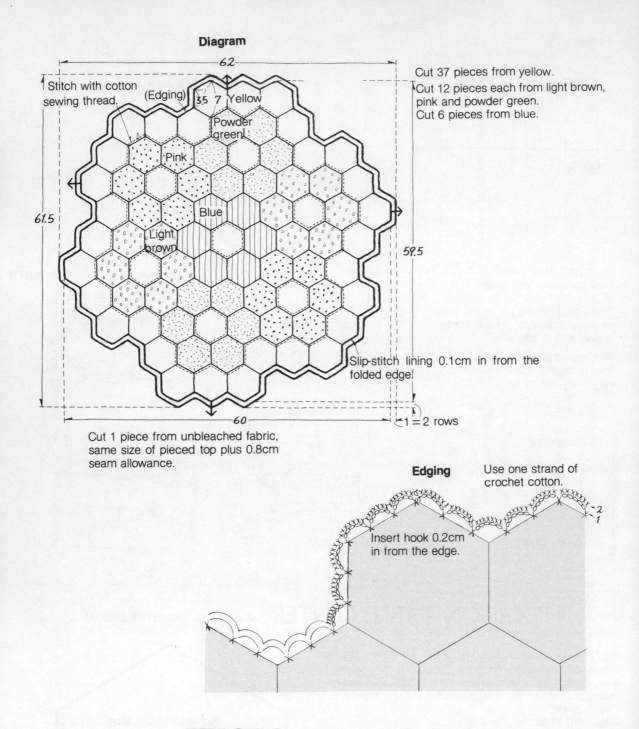

62

Stitch with cotton
sewing thread.

(Edging) 35 7 Yellow

Cut 37 pieces from yellow.
Cut 12 pieces each from light brown,
pink and powder green.
Cut 6 pieces from blue.

Powder
green

Pink

Blue

61.5

59.5

Light
brown

Slip-stitch lining 0.1cm in from the
folded edge.

60

1 = 2 rows

Cut 1 piece from unbleached fabric,
same size of pieced top plus 0.8cm
seam allowance.

Edging   Use one strand of
crochet cotton.

Insert hook 0.2cm
in from the edge.

2
1

PILLOWS, shown on pages 16 and 17

MATERIALS: Cotton fabrics (See the photo for designs.): For Pillow at left: white, 90cm by 44cm; olive green, 28cm square; dark brown and red, 28cm by 14cm each. For Pillow at right: yellow, 90cm by 44cm; red, 28cm square; olive green and dark brown, 28cm by 14cm each. #50 beige cotton sewing thread. For one pillow: one zipper, 38cm long; fabric for inner pillow, 90cm by 46cm; kapok, 300g.
FINISHED SIZE: 42cm square

DIRECTIONS:
1. Cut out pieces for Front, adding seam allowance all around. Sew pieces of block together, using method C on page 105. Turn seams to one side. Join blocks together.
2. Cut out pieces for Back. Sew zipper in place.
3. With right sides of Front and Back together, stitch all around. Turn to right side. Insert inner pillow.

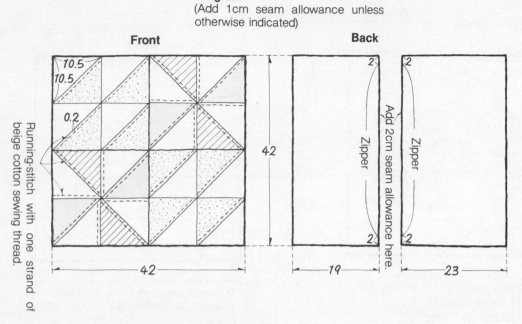

Front

10.5
10.5
0.2

Running-stitch with one strand of beige cotton sewing thread.

42

42

Back

2
2
2
2

Add 2cm seam allowance here.

Zipper

Zipper

19

23

Color Key and Required Number of Pieces

	Left	Right	Pieces
	White	Yellow	16
	Olive green	Red	8
	Dark brown	Dark brown	4
	Red	Olive green	4
Back	White	Yellow	

Running Stitch

4 3 2 1
in out in out

PINCUSHIONS, shown on page 18

MATERIALS: Cotton fabrics: For 1: floral prints in the following colors: dark brown, 19cm by 15cm; red, yellow, white and olive green, 5.5cm square each. For 2 and 5: See the list on next page. For 3: blue, 9.5cm by 14cm; dark blue and yellow green, 9.5cm square each; beige with small flowers, 11.5cm square. For 4: prints with climbing plants in the following colors: olive green, 18cm by 14cm; unbleached and red, 12cm by 9cm each. For 6: floral prints in the following colors: yellow green, light reddish brown, brown with beige, light brown, dark red, light olive green, brown with white, gray, navy blue, 4.5cm square each; orange, 10.5cm square. #50 white cotton sewing thread for 4. Cotton batting.

FINISHED SIZE: See the diagrams.

DIRECTIONS:

For 1: Cut out pieces, adding seam allowance. Sew pieces together, using method B on page 104. Turn seams to one side. With right sides of pieced Front and Back together, stitch all around leaving an opening. Turn to right side. Stuff with cotton batting. Slip-stitch opening closed.

For 2 and 5: Cut out pieces, adding seam allowance. Sew pieces together following the diagram. Make up for pincushion in same manner as 1.

For 3: Cut out pieces, adding seam allowance. Sew triangles together, using method A on page 102. Sew pieced triangles and strips for border, using method B on page 104. Make up for pincushion in same manner as 1.

For 4: Cut out pieces, adding seam allowance. Sew pieces (A) and (B) together, using method B on page 104. Turn seams to (A) side. Sew pieces (B) and (C) together and turn seams to (B) side. Sew other pieces together in this way. Make up for pincushion in same manner as 1.

For 5: Following the diagram, sew pieces together, using method B on page 104. Make up for pincushion in same manner as 1.

Diagram
(Add 0.7cm seam allowance)

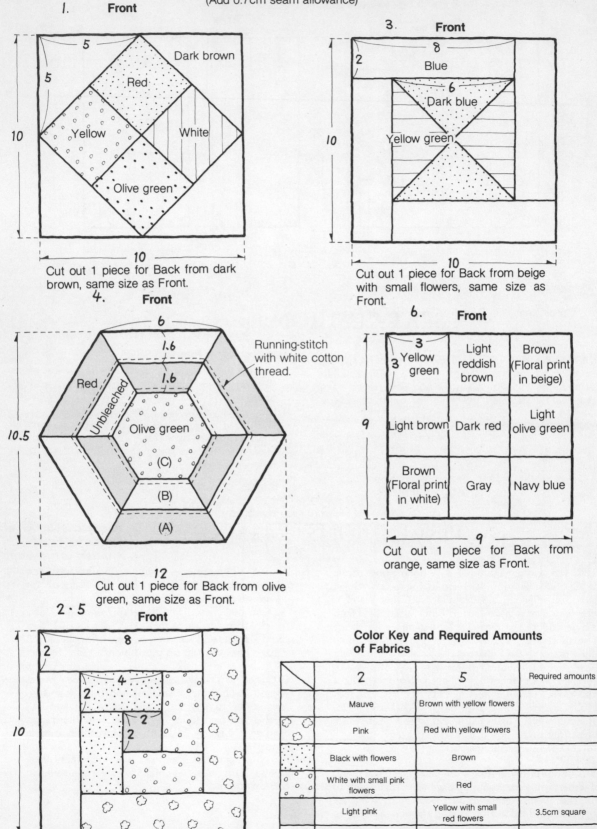

1. **Front**

5
5
Dark brown
Red
5
10
Yellow
White
Olive green
10

Cut out 1 piece for Back from dark brown, same size as Front.

3. **Front**

8
2
Blue
6
Dark blue
10
Yellow green
10

Cut out 1 piece for Back from beige with small flowers, same size as Front.

4. **Front**

6
1.6
1.6
Red
Unbleached
10.5
Olive green
(C)
(B)
(A)
12

Running-stitch with white cotton thread.

Cut out 1 piece for Back from olive green, same size as Front.

6. **Front**

3
3 Yellow green | Light reddish brown | Brown (Floral print in beige)
9
Light brown | Dark red | Light olive green
Brown (Floral print in white) | Gray | Navy blue
9

Cut out 1 piece for Back from orange, same size as Front.

2·5 **Front**

8
2
4
2
2
2
10
10

Color Key and Required Amounts of Fabrics

	2	5	Required amounts
	Mauve	Brown with yellow flowers	
	Pink	Red with yellow flowers	
	Black with flowers	Brown	
	White with small pink flowers	Red	
	Light pink	Yellow with small red flowers	3.5cm square
Back	Black with flowers	〃	11.5cm square

66

To Join Pieces for 2 and 5 Pincushions

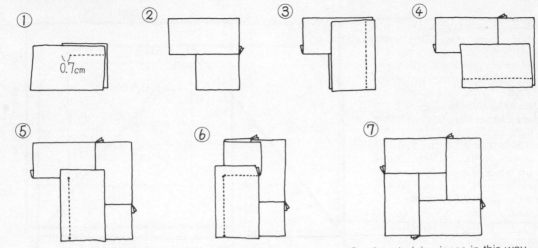

Continue to join pieces in this way.

SEAT CUSHION, shown on page 22

MATERIALS FOR ONE CUSHION: Cotton fabrics (See the photo for colors and designs.): 90cm by 16cm each for (a) and (b); 75cm by 47cm for (c). One zipper, 41cm long. Fabric for inner pillow, 49cm by 96cm. Kapok, 180g.
FINISHED SIZE: 45cm square

DIRECTIONS:
1. Cut out pieces, adding seam allowance. Sew pieces together, following piecing instructions (A) and (B) below.
2. Cut out pieces for Back. Sew zipper in place.
3. With right sides of Front and Back together, stitch all around. Turn to right side.
4. Make inner cushion and stuff with kapok flatly. Insert inner cushion.

Diagram

Front

Back
(Add 0.7cm seam allowance unless otherwise indicated)

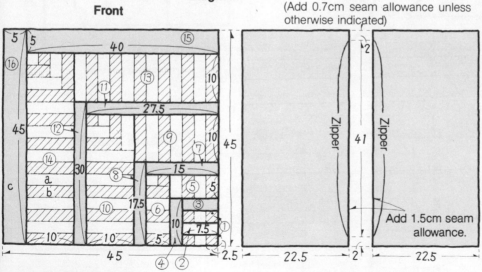

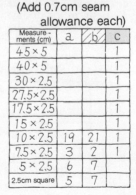

Add 1.5cm seam allowance.

Required Number of Pieces for Front
(Add 0.7cm seam allowance each)

Measurements (cm)	a	b	c
45 × 5			1
40 × 5			1
30 × 2.5			1
27.5 × 2.5			1
17.5 × 2.5			1
15 × 2.5			1
10 × 2.5	19	21	1
7.5 × 2.5	3	2	1
5 × 2.5	6	7	
2.5cm square	5	7	

Instructions for Front:
(A) With right sides facing, machine-stitch pieces between bold lines together—pieces of 1, 5, 6, 9, 10, 13 and 14. (To sew pieces of 6, 10 and 14, join smaller pieces first.)

(B) Join pieces as numbered from 1 through 16.

Turn all seams to one side.

POTHOLDERS, shown on page 19

MATERIALS: Cotton fabrics: For 1: red brown, 40cm square; gray, 12cm square; unbleached, 7cm square; navy with white flowers, 9.5cm by 4cm. For 2: yellow with red flowers, 40cm square; red with yellow flowers, 12cm square; white with red flowers, 9.5cm by 4cm. For 3: olive green, 40cm square; light olive green with white flowers, light reddish brown with white flowers, 9cm by 7cm each; mustard, 7cm square; brown, 9.5cm by 4cm. For 4: brown with white flowers, 40cm square; light yellow brown, 12cm square; dark red with orange flowers, 10cm by 7cm; mustard and red brown, 3.5cm by 7cm each. For 5: red with yellow flowers, 40cm square; blue, 12cm square; white with red flowers, 7cm square; dark brown with pink flowers, 9.5cm by 4cm. #50 cotton sewing thread and #25 six-strand embroidery floss (See the list below for colors.). Quilt batting and interlining fabric for one potholder, 9.5cm by 14cm each.

FINISHED SIZE: 14.5cm by 9.5cm
DIRECTIONS:
1. Cut out pieces, adding seam allowance.
2. Sew pieces of (d) (e) (f) and (g) together, using method B on page 104. Press seams of (e) and (f) open. Turn other seams toward center.
3. Sew pieces of (a) (c) and (b) together. Turn seams toward center.
4. Sew 2, 3 and (h) pieces together. Turn seams to (c) and (h) sides.
5. Embroider windows in running stitch for 1 and 5 potholders.
6. Place pieced top, batting and interlining together, quilt along quilting lines shown in the diagram.
7. Place quilted piece on lining. Make hanging loop. Bind edges with bias-cut strip, catching ends of loop in place.

Patterns (Actual Size) (Add 0.7cm seam allowance)

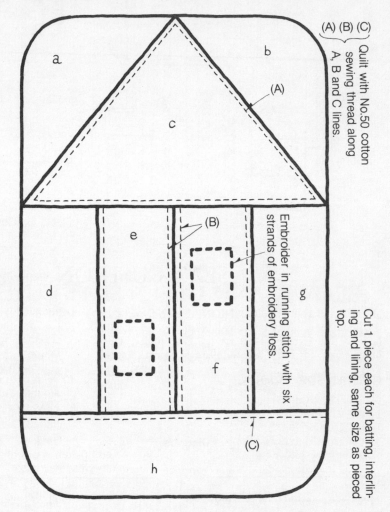

Quilt with No.50 cotton sewing thread along A, B and C lines.

Embroider in running stitch with six strands of embroidery floss.

Cut 1 piece each for batting, interlining and lining, same size as pieced top.

Color Key

		1	2	3	4	5
Patch pieces	a	Gray	Red with yellow flowers	Light olive green with white flowers	Light yellow brown	Blue
	b	Gray	Red with yellow flowers	Light reddish brown with white flowers	Light yellow brown	Blue
	c	Red brown	Yellow with red flowers	Olive green	Dark red with orange flowers	Red with yellow flowers
	d	Gray	Red with yellow flowers	Mustard	Light yellow brown	Blue
	e	Unbleached	Yellow with red flowers	Light olive green with white flowers	Mustard	White with red flowers
	f	Unbleached	Yellow with red flowers	Light reddish brown with white flowers	Red brown	White with red flowers
	g	Gray	Red with yellow flowers	Mustard	Light yellow brown	Blue
	h	Navy with white flowers	White with red flowers	Brown	Brown with white flowers	Dark brown with pink flowers
No.50 cotton sewing thread	(A)	Beige	Red	Beige	Beige	Red
	(B)	White	Red	Beige	Beige	White
	(C)	White	Red	Beige	Beige	Dark brown
Thread for Running stitch		Dark brown				Blue
Strip for binding, Lining & Hanging loop		Red brown	Yellow with red flowers	Olive green	Brown with white flowers	Red with yellow flowers

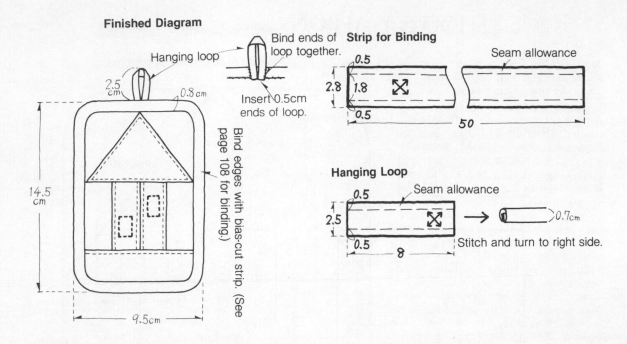

Finished Diagram

Hanging loop

Bind ends of loop together.

2.5 cm

0.8 cm

Insert 0.5cm ends of loop.

14.5 cm

9.5cm

Bind edges with bias-cut strip. (See page 108 for binding.)

Strip for Binding

Seam allowance

0.5

2.8   1.8

0.5

50

Hanging Loop

0.5

Seam allowance

2.5

0.5

8

0.7cm

Stitch and turn to right side.

BROWN AND GREEN SEAT CUSHIONS, shown on page 23

MATERIALS FOR ONE CUSHION: Cotton fabrics (See the photo for colors and designs.): 80cm by 12cm each for (a) and (b); 84cm by 47cm for (c). #25 six-strand embroidery floss in dark brown for Cushion at left, olive green for Cushion at right. One zipper, 40cm long. Fabric for inner cushion, 49cm by 96cm. Kapok, 180g.
FINISHED SIZE: 45cm square
DIRECTIONS:
1. Cut out 16 pieces each for (a) and (b), 4 pieces for (c), adding seam allowance.

2. Following the diagram, sew pieces together, using method C on page 105. Press seams open. Embroider in running stitch along dash lines shown in the diagram, using four strands of embroidory floss in needle.
3. Cut out pieces for Back. Sew zipper in place.
4. With right sides of Front and Back together, stitch all around. Turn to right side.
5. Make inner cushion. Insert inner cushion.

Diagram
(Add 1cm seam allowance unless otherwise indicated)

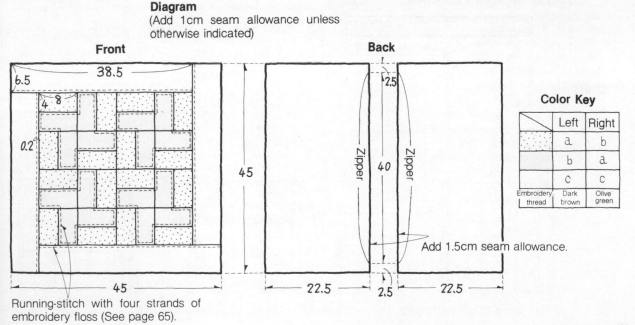

Front

6.5

38.5

4 8

0.2

45

45

Back

2.5

Zipper

40

Zipper

22.5

2.5

22.5

Add 1.5cm seam allowance.

Color Key

	Left	Right
	a	b
	b	a
	c	c
Embroidery thread	Dark brown	Olive green

Running-stitch with four strands of embroidery floss (See page 65).

69

SHOO-FLY APRON, shown on page 24, left

MATERIALS: Cotton fabrics: light brown, 90cm by 84cm; blue gray with beige flowers, 90cm by 22cm. #25 six-strand embroidery floss in brown.

FINISHED SIZE: See the diagram.

Cutting Diagrams

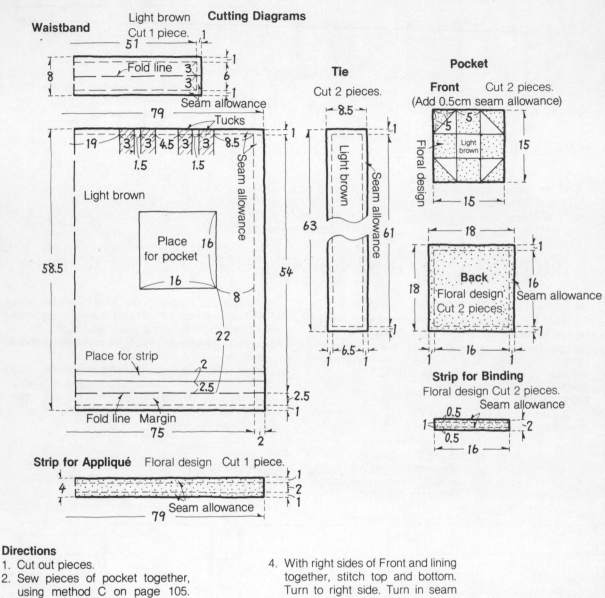

Waistband
Light brown
Cut 1 piece.
51
1
Fold line 3
3
8
79
6
1
1
Seam allowance

Tucks
19 3 3 4.5 3 3 8.5
1.5 1.5
Light brown
Seam allowance
1
Place for pocket 16
16
58.5
54
8
22
Place for strip
2
2.5
2.5
Fold line Margin
75
1
2

Tie
Cut 2 pieces.
8.5
Light brown
Seam allowance
63
61
1
1
6.5
1 1

Pocket
Front Cut 2 pieces.
(Add 0.5cm seam allowance)
Floral design
5
5
Light brown
15
15

18
Back
Floral design
Cut 2 pieces.
1
18
16
Seam allowance
1
1 16 1

Strip for Binding
Floral design Cut 2 pieces.
Seam allowance
0.5
1
2
0.5
16

Strip for Appliqué Floral design Cut 1 piece.
4
1
2
1
79
Seam allowance

Directions
1. Cut out pieces.
2. Sew pieces of pocket together, using method C on page 105. Press seams open.
3. Bind edges of sides with strips.

4. With right sides of Front and lining together, stitch top and bottom. Turn to right side. Turn in seam allowance of each side.

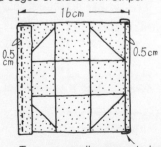

16cm
0.5 cm
0.5 cm
Turn seam allowance to back.

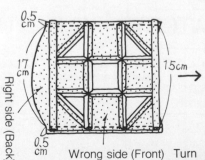

0.5 cm
17 cm
Right side (Back)
15 cm
0.5 cm
Wrong side (Front)

Machine-stitch in the ditch.
0.5 cm

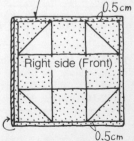

Right side (Front)
0.5 cm
Turn excess to back, showing 0.5cm from seams.

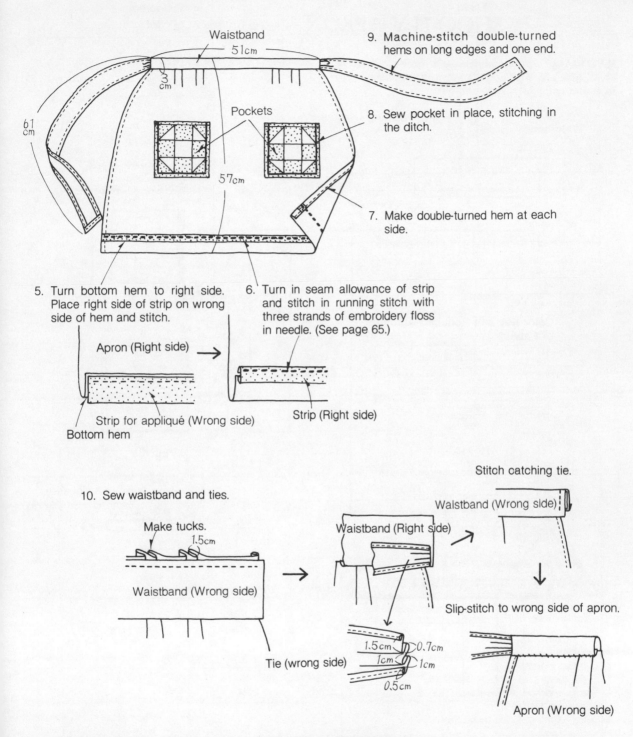

Waistband
51cm
3cm
61cm
57cm

Pockets

9. Machine-stitch double-turned hems on long edges and one end.

8. Sew pocket in place, stitching in the ditch.

7. Make double-turned hem at each side.

5. Turn bottom hem to right side. Place right side of strip on wrong side of hem and stitch.

Apron (Right side) →

Strip for appliqué (Wrong side)
Bottom hem

6. Turn in seam allowance of strip and stitch in running stitch with three strands of embroidery floss in needle. (See page 65.)

Strip (Right side)

10. Sew waistband and ties.

Make tucks.
1.5cm
Waistband (Wrong side)

Tie (wrong side)
1.5cm 0.7cm
1cm   1cm
0.5cm

Waistband (Right side)

Stitch catching tie.
Walstband (Wrong side)

Slip-stitch to wrong side of apron.

Apron (Wrong side)

SMALL PATCHWORK PICTURES, shown on pages 30 and 31

MATERIALS: Cotton fabrics (See the list on next page.). Cotton fabric for lining, 16.5cm square for one picture. White cotton sewing thread.
FINISHED SIZE: 15cm square

DIRECTIONS:
1. Cut out pieces, adding 0.7cm seam allowance. Sew pieces together, using method B on page 104. Press seams open.
2. Place pieced picture on lining and stitch along stitching lines shown in the diagram.

Yacht

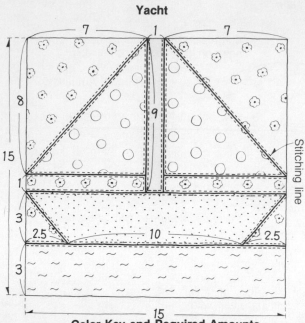

Color Key and Required Amounts of Fabrics

⊙ Yellow with white dots and flowers	14.5cm×15.5cm
○ Sky blue with white dots	9.5cm×10.5cm
Cobalt blue	2.5cm×10.5cm
White and blue checks	18cm×4.5cm
~ Blue and yellow-green stripes	16.5cm×4.5cm

Schoolhouse

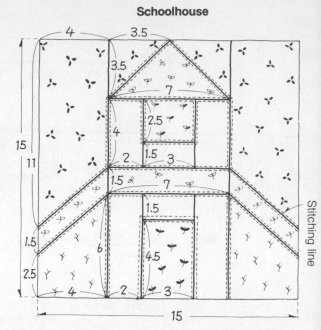

⋎ Sky blue with flowers	17cm×13.5cm
✿ Brown with flowers	11cm×16cm
⋎ Blue with flowers	4.5cm×4cm
⋟ Turquoise blue with flowers	4.5cm×6cm
White with flowers	14cm×11.5cm
Y Beige with flowers	11cm×8.5cm

House

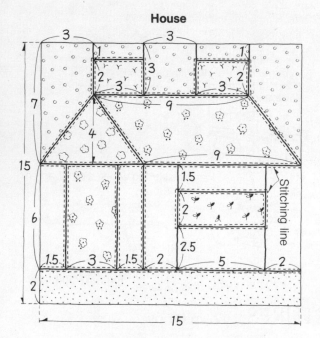

°° Pink with white dots	13.5cm×8.5cm
♡ Yellow with white flowers	9cm×6cm
Y Olive green with flowers	4.5cm×7cm
✿ Red with yellow flowers	19.5cm×7.5cm
✿ Blue with flowers	6.5cm×3.5cm
White with lavender and orange flowers	19.5cm×7.5cm
∷ White and green checks	16.5cm×3.5cm

Fir

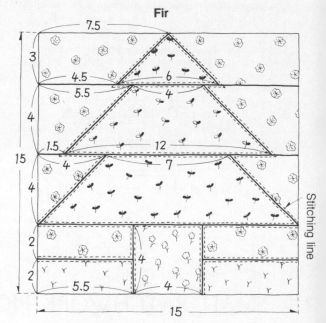

✾ White with pink flowers	20cm×16.5cm
❦ Turquoise blue with flowers	18cm×10.5cm
⋎ Blue with flowers	15cm×5.5cm
⋄ Dark brown with yellow flowers	5.5cm Square
Y Olive green with flowers	7cm Square

Tulip

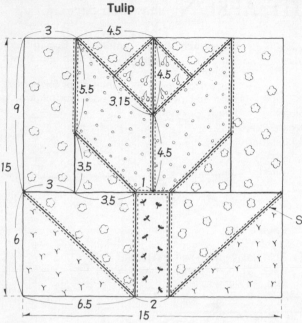

Color Key and Required Amounts of Fabrics

	Yellow with white flowers	24cm×11.5cm
	Pink with white dots	12cm×11.5cm
	Off-white with cherries	5.5cm Square
	Turquoise blue with flowers	3.5cm×7.5cm
	Olive green with flowers	9cm×8.5cm

Stitching line

STRIPED PILLOWS, shown on pages 28 and 29

MATERIALS: Cotton fabrics (See the photo for colors and designs.): For Pillow at left: 22cm by 11cm each for (a) (b) (f) (g) (h)and (i); 11cm square each for (c) (d) (e) (j) (k) and (l); dark brown, 63cm by 42cm. For Pillow at right; 22cm by 11cm each for (c) (i) (m) (n) (o) and (p); 11cm square each for (b) (f) (j) (l) (g) (r) and (s); dark brown, 63cm by 42cm. One zipper, 34cm long. Fabric for inner pillow, 84cm by 43cm. Kapok, 420g.
FINISHED SIZE: 39cm square

DIRECTIONS:
1. Cut out pieces as indicated. Sew pieces together, using method C on page 105. Press seams open.
2. Sew strips for border to pieced Front.
3. Cut out pieces for Back. Sew zipper in place. With right sides of Front and Back together, stitch all around. Turn to right side.
4. Insert inner pillow.

Diagram
Front (Add 0.8cm seam allowance unless otherwise indicated)

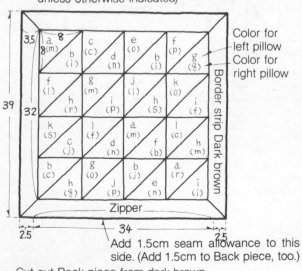

Color for left pillow
Color for right pillow

Add 1.5cm seam allowance to this side. (Add 1.5cm to Back piece, too.)

Cut out Back piece from dark brown fabric, same size as Front.

Required Number of Pieces

Left pillow

Cut 4 pieces each from (b) and (h).
Cut 3 pieces each from (a) (f) (g) and (i).
Cut 2 pieces each from (c) (d) (e) (j) (k) and (l).
Cut 4 pieces for border strips.

Right pillow

Cut 4 pieces from (m).
Cut 3 pieces each from (c) (i) (n) (o) and (p).
Cut 2 pieces each from (f) (j) (l) (q) (r) and (s).
Cut 1 piece from (b).
Cut 4 pieces for border strips.

NAVY AND WHITE APRON, shown on page 25

MATERIALS: Medium weight cotton fabrics: unbleached, 37cm by 150cm; navy blue, 37cm by 144cm; 1 skein of #25 six-strand embroidery floss in off-white.
FINISHED SIZE: 41cm wide and 69cm long
DIRECTIONS:
1. Cut out patches adding seam allowance. Sew pieces together, using method C on page 105. Turn seams to navy fabric side.

2. Using three strands of embroidery floss in needle, embroider in running stitch along dash lines shown in the diagram.
3. Cut out one piece for lining, strips for border, waistband and ties. Make up for apron following instructions (A) through (F).

Diagram
(Add 0.7cm seam allowance to patches. See Cutting diagram for border and ties.)

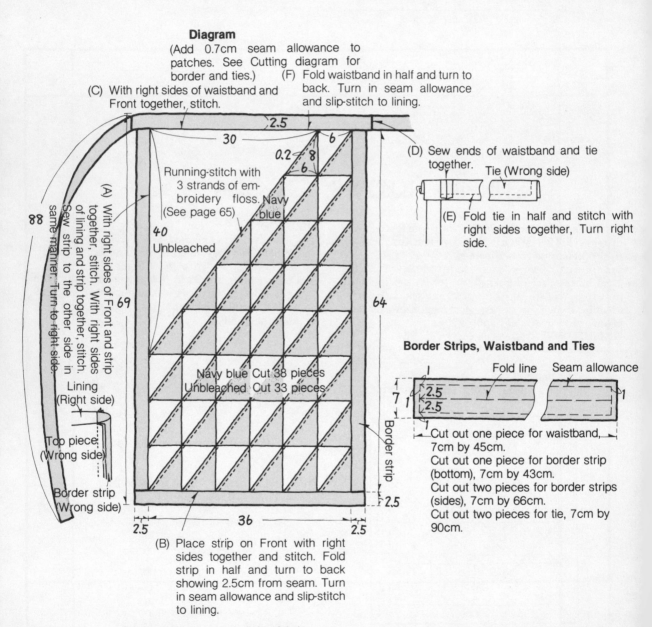

(C) With right sides of waistband and Front together, stitch.

(F) Fold waistband in half and turn to back. Turn in seam allowance and slip-stitch to lining.

2.5

30

6

0.2 8

6

(A) With right sides of Front and strip together, stitch. With right sides of lining and strip together, stitch. Sew strip to the other side in same manner. Turn to right side.

Running-stitch with 3 strands of embroidery floss. (See page 65)

Navy blue

40
Unbleached

88

69

64

(D) Sew ends of waistband and tie together.

Tie (Wrong side)

(E) Fold tie in half and stitch with right sides together, Turn right side.

Lining (Right side)

Top piece (Wrong side)

Border strip (Wrong side)

Navy blue Cut 38 pieces
Unbleached Cut 33 pieces

Border strip

2.5

Border Strips, Waistband and Ties

Fold line   Seam allowance

7

2.5
2.5

Cut out one piece for waistband, 7cm by 45cm.
Cut out one piece for border strip (bottom), 7cm by 43cm.
Cut out two pieces for border strips (sides), 7cm by 66cm.
Cut out two pieces for tie, 7cm by 90cm.

2.5   36   2.5

(B) Place strip on Front with right sides together and stitch. Fold strip in half and turn to back showing 2.5cm from seam. Turn in seam allowance and slip-stitch to lining.

Cut out one piece from lining fabric, 37cm by 65cm.

NINE-PATCH TABLECLOTH, shown on pages 26 and 27

MATERIALS: Cotton fabrics (See the photo for colors and designs.): 90cm by 104cm for (a); 90cm by 53cm for (b); 90cm by 1m for (c); 124cm square for lining.
FINISHED SIZE: 122cm square

DIRECTIONS:
1. Cut out pieces, adding 0.7cm seam allowance all around. Sew pieces together, using method C on page 105. Press seams open.
2. With right sides of pieced top and lining together, stitch all around leaving an opening. Turn to right side. Slip-stitch opening closed.
3. Machine-stitch in the ditch diagonally in both ways.

a_1 = Cut 64 pieces.
a_2, c_1, c_4 = Cut 4 pieces each.
b = Cut 80 pieces.
C_2 = Cut 12 pieces.
C_3 = Cut 9 pieces.

Diagram

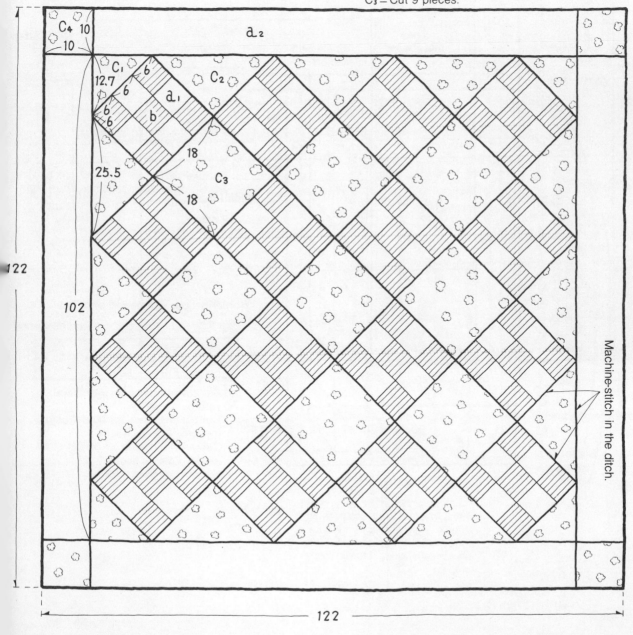

75

PINWHEEL APRON, shown on page 24, right

MATERIALS: Cotton fabrics: yellow-brown, 90cm by 122cm; dark brown, 90cm by 13cm; light brown, 90cm by 10cm. #25 six-strand embroidery floss in dark brown and brown.

FINISHED SIZE: 80cm long

Cutting Diagrams
Use yellow-brown fabric otherwise indicated.

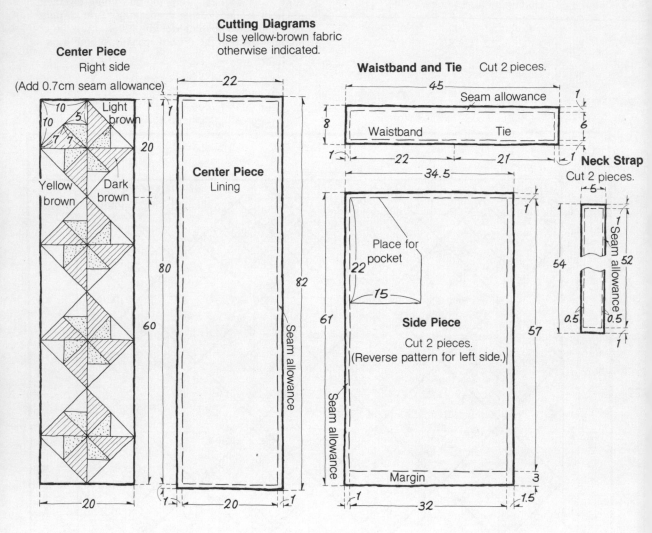

Center Piece
Right side
(Add 0.7cm seam allowance)

10 10 5
7 7
Light brown
Yellow brown   Dark brown
20
80
60
20

Center Piece
Lining
22
1
82
Seam allowance
1 20 1

Waistband and Tie   Cut 2 pieces.
45
Seam allowance
8   Waistband   Tie
1   22   21   1
1 6

Neck Strap
Cut 2 pieces.
5
1
54   52
0.5 0.5
1
Seam allowance

34.5
22   Place for pocket
15
61
Side Piece
Cut 2 pieces.
(Reverse pattern for left side.)
1
57
Seam allowance
Margin   3
1   32   1.5

Pocket Cut 2 pieces. (Reverse pattern for left side.)

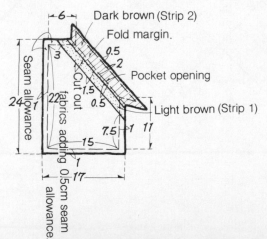

6
Dark brown (Strip 2)
Fold margin.
0.5
3   2
Cut out   Pocket opening
1.5
22
0.5   Light brown (Strip 1)
24
Seam allowance
7.5 1 11
15
fabrics adding 0.5cm seam allowance.
1
17

76

Directions

1. Cut out pieces, adding seam allowance all around.
2. Sew pieces together to make center piece using method C on page 105. Press seams open. Half-back stitch along dash lines shown in the diagram with one strand of embroidery floss in colors to match fabrics.

Half-back stitch 0.2cm in from seams.

Seam allowance

3. Make pockets.

Half-back stitch

Right side

(A) Sew strips 1 and 2 to pocket opening side. Turn seams to strip side.

Strips 1   Strips 2
1.5 cm   0.5 cm

(D) Fold seam allowance to wrong side.

(B) Half-back stitch 0.2cm in from seams with one strand of embroidery floss in matching color.

(C) Turn strip to back showing 0.5cm on front. Turn in seam allowance and slip-stitch to wrong side.

4.

(F) Fold waistband in half, turn in seam allowance and slip-stitch to wrong side.

(E) Place pocket on gathered side. Place waistband as shown, with top edge of pocket in between. Stitch.

Tie

22cm

21cm   Slip-stitch

(D) Run a gathering stitch across top edge of each side. Pull thread to fit 22cm.

(C) Sew pocket here.

(A) Machine-stitch double-turned hem.

(B) Slip-stitch double-turned hem at the bottom.

6. Make neck strap.

Turn in seam allowance of end and slip-stitch.

With right sides together, fold in half and stitch. Turn to right side. Bring seam to center and press seam open.

53 cm

2 cm

7.

Neck strap

1cm

(A) With right sides of Front and lining together and neck strap in between, stitch. Turn to right side.

80 cm

Wrong side

Lining (Right side)

(B) Turn in seam allowance and slip-stitch to wrong side.

Bottom

(C) Slip-stitch end of lining to wrong side, 0.5cm in from the folded edge.

5. Sew center piece to skirt. Turn seams to center piece.

20cm

3cm

ROSE GARDEN BEDSPREAD, shown on pages 32 and 33

MATERIALS: Cotton fabrics (See the list below for (a) (b) (c) and (d).): navy blue, 80cm by 546cm; light-weight sheeting, 92cm by 916cm.
FINISHED SIZE: 276cm by 200cm

Diagram

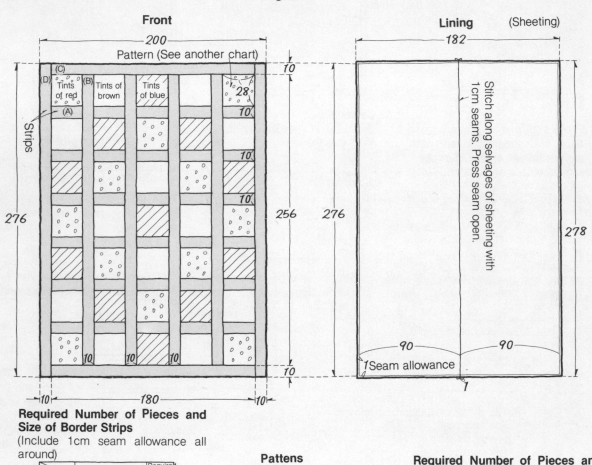

Front

200
Pattern (See another chart)

(C)
(D) Tints of red (B) Tints of brown Tints of blue 28
(A)
10

Strips

276   256   10   10   10

10   180   10

Lining   (Sheeting)

182

Stitch along selvages of sheeting with 1cm seams. Press seam open.

276   278

90   90

1 Seam allowance   1

Required Number of Pieces and Size of Border Strips
(Include 1cm seam allowance all around)

		Width×Length (cm)	Required pieces
Navy blue	(A)	12 × 30	30
	(B)	12 × 258	4
	(C)	12 × 182	2
	(D)	22 × 278	2

Pattens
(Add 1cm seam allowance)

28

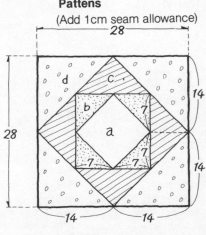

d   c
b
a
7
7   7   7

28

14   14

14   14

Required Number of Pieces and Amounts of Fabrics
(See the photo for colors and designs.)

Pattern	Color	Pieces	Required amounts
Tints of red Cut 12 pieces	a	12	72 × 24
	b	48	84 × 32
	c	48	81 × 54
	d	48	88cm square
Tints of brown Cut 12 pieces	a	12	72 × 24
	b	48	84 × 32
	c	48	81 × 54
	d	48	88cm Square
Tints of blue Cut 11 pieces	a	11	72 × 24
	b	44	84 × 32
	c	44	81 × 54
	d	44	88cm square

Directions

1. Cut out pieces, adding seam allowance.

2.

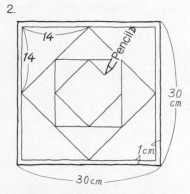

Cut out 35 pieces, 30cm square each, from sheeting. Transfer the pattern to right side of sheeting.

3.

Center piece (a) on sheeting. Baste (a) to sheeting as shown. Mark corners of (a).

4.

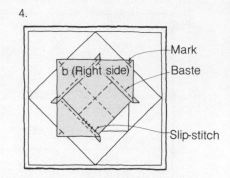

Turn in seam allowance of (b). Place (b) on (a) matching marks and baste. After basting four pieces, slip-stitch (b) to (a), catching sheeting. Mark corners of (b).

6. Cut out required number of border strips shown in the list. With right sides together, sew border strip to each block in alphabetical order. Join strips (A) to blocks. Then join rows of blocks with strips (B). Sew top and bottom strips (C) as shown. Finish with strips (D). Turn seams to strip.

5. Sew pieces (c) and (d) in same manner. Make indicated number of blocks in tints of red, brown and blue indivisually.

7. With right sides of pieced top and lining together, stitch along each side. Turn to right side.

8. Turn in seam allowances of top and bottom. Stitch all around.

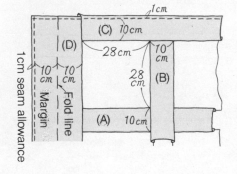

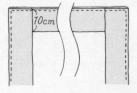

OHIO STAR PILLOWS, shown on pages 34 and 35

MATERIALS: Cotton fabrics (See the photo for colors and designs.): 90cm by 10cm for (a); 60cm by 27cm for (b); 81cm by 51cm for (c). #25 six-strand embroidery floss: small amount each of dark and light moss green, mauve, lavender, cream and bright yellow for Green Pillow at right; small amount each of dark and light moss green, rose pink, mauve and cream for Pink Pillow at left. One zipper, 43cm long. Fabric for inner pillow, 49cm by 96cm. Kapok, 400g.
FINISHED SIZE: 45cm square

DIRECTIONS:

1. Cut out pieces for Front, adding 1cm seam allowance all around. Cut out pieces for Back, adding seam allowance as indicated.
2. Trace actual size pattern for embroidery and transfer design to center piece of Front. Embroider as indicated.
3. Sew pieces together, using method C on page 105. Press seams open.
4. Sew zipper to Back pieces.
5. With right sides of Front and Back together, stitch all around. Turn to right side. Insert inner pillow.

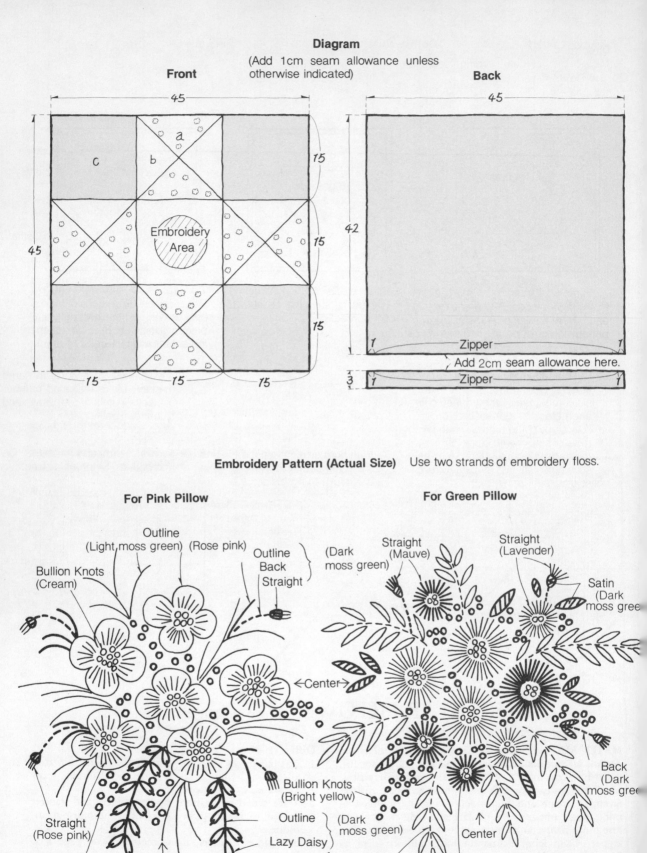

Diagram

(Add 1cm seam allowance unless otherwise indicated)

Front

45

15

15

15

45

15 15 15

a

b

c

Embroidery
Area

Back

45

42

Zipper

Add 2cm seam allowance here.

1 1

3
1 Zipper 1

Embroidery Pattern (Actual Size) Use two strands of embroidery floss.

For Pink Pillow

Outline
(Light moss green) (Rose pink)

Bullion Knots
(Cream)

Outline
Back
Straight

←Center→

Bullion Knots
(Bright yellow)

Outline (Dark
moss green)

Lazy Daisy

Straight
(Rose pink)

Bullion Knots
(Mauve)

Center

(Light moss green)

For Green Pillow

(Dark
moss green)

Straight
(Mauve)

Straight
(Lavender)

Satin
(Dark
moss green)

Back
(Dark
moss green)

↑
Center

Back
Satin

Bullion Knots
(Cream)

Straight Stitch

Outline Stitch

Back Stitch

Satin Stitch

Lazy Daisy Stitch

Bullion Knot

CRIB QUILT, shown on pages 36 and 37

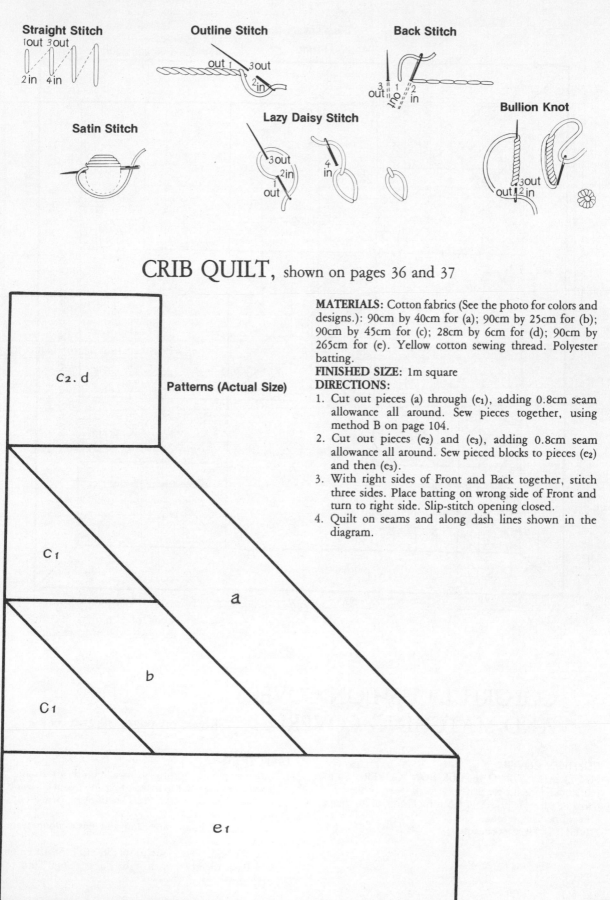

Patterns (Actual Size)

MATERIALS: Cotton fabrics (See the photo for colors and designs.): 90cm by 40cm for (a); 90cm by 25cm for (b); 90cm by 45cm for (c); 28cm by 6cm for (d); 90cm by 265cm for (e). Yellow cotton sewing thread. Polyester batting.

FINISHED SIZE: 1m square

DIRECTIONS:

1. Cut out pieces (a) through (e₁), adding 0.8cm seam allowance all around. Sew pieces together, using method B on page 104.
2. Cut out pieces (e₂) and (e₃), adding 0.8cm seam allowance all around. Sew pieced blocks to pieces (e₂) and then (e₃).
3. With right sides of Front and Back together, stitch three sides. Place batting on wrong side of Front and turn to right side. Slip-stitch opening closed.
4. Quilt on seams and along dash lines shown in the diagram.

a · b = Cut 40 pieces each.
c_1 = Cut 80 pieces.
$c_2 · e_1$ = Cut 20 pieces each.
d = Cut 5 pieces.
$e_2 · e_3$ = Cut 4 pieces each.

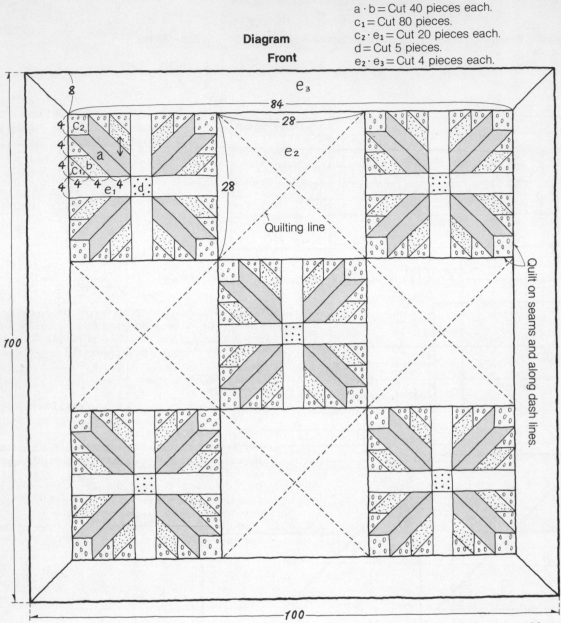

8

e_3

84

28

C_2

4

4

a

4

c_1

b

4

4

4

e_1

4

d

e_2

28

28

Quilting line

100

Quilt on seams and along dash lines.

100

Sew 2 pieces of 52cm by 102cm together to make 102cm square for lining.

COLORFUL CUSHION COVERS AND MATCHING COVERLET, shown on pages 38 and 39

CUSHION COVER
MATERIALS FOR ONE CUSHION COVER: Cotton fabrics (See the list for patches.): dark green or wine red, 65cm by 62cm; light weight fabric for lining, 62cm square. One zipper, 50cm long.
FINISHED SIZE: 60cm square

DIRECTIONS:
1. Cut out pieces, adding seam allowance all around. Sew pieces together to make group A, B and C, using method B on page 104. Press seams open. Sew groups together.
2. Place pieced Front on lining and baste along seam lines.
3. Cut out Back pieces. Sew zipper in place. Stitch Front and Back together, with right sides facing. Turn to right side.

Diagram

(Add 1cm seam allowance unless otherwise indicated)

Front

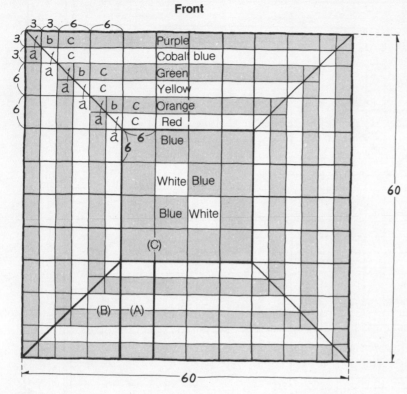

Required Number of Pieces and Amounts of Fabrics

		Required pieces	Required amounts (cm)
Purple	a	8	90 × 22
	b	8	
	c	32	
Cobalt blue	a	8	90 × 22
	c	32	
Green	a	8	90 × 17
	b	8	
	c	24	
Yellow	a	8	90 × 17
	c	24	
Orange	a	8	90 × 17
	b	8	
	c	16	
Red	a	8	90 × 12
	c	16	
Blue		14	90 × 16
White		2	16 × 8

Back

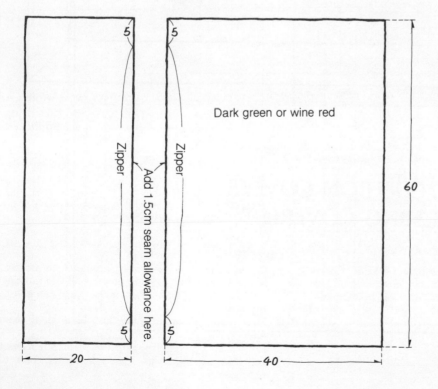

Dark green or wine red

COVERLET

Diagram

Front   (Add 1cm seam allowance)

For center piece, see the list for Cushion Cover.

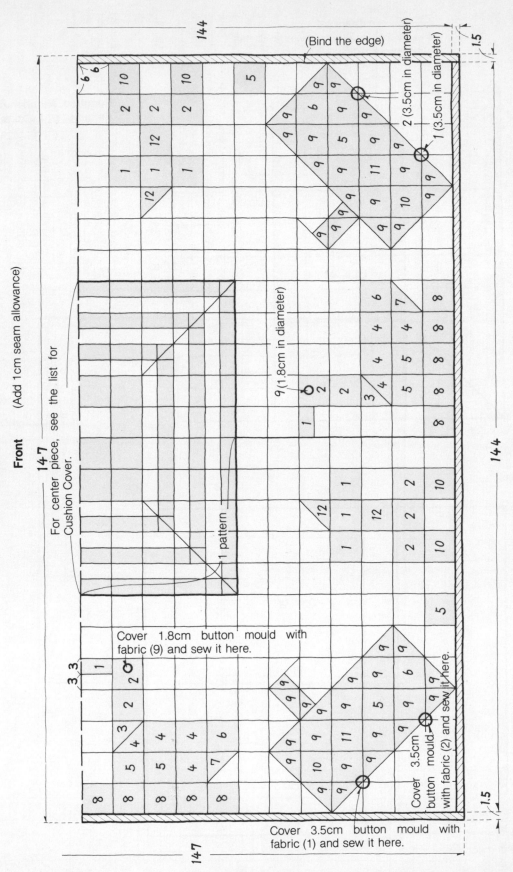

(Bind the edge)

144

147

144

1.5

1.5

2 (3.5cm in diameter)

1 (3.5cm in diameter)

9 (1.8cm in diameter)

1 pattern

Cover 1.8cm button mould with fabric (9) and sew it here.

Cover 3.5cm button mould with fabric (2) and sew it here.

Cover 3.5cm button mould with fabric (1) and sew it here.

84

Color Key and Required Number of Pieces except for Center Square.

No.	Color	Figure	Required pieces
1	Yellow	□	4
		□	12
2	Green	□	20
3	Wine red	△	4
4	White	△	4
		□	12
5	Pink	□	16
6	Orange	□	8
7	Dark green	△	4
8	Blue	□	20
		Small □	8
9	Navy blue	△	52
		□	24
10	Red	□	12
11	Purple	△	4
12	Cobalt blue	△	4
		Small □	8
	Beige	△	60
		□	4
		□	272

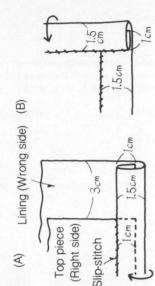

To Neaten Corner

(A) Lining (Wrong side) (B)

Top piece (Right side)

Slip-stitch

3cm

1cm

1.5cm

1cm

1.5cm

1cm

MATERIALS FOR COVERLET: Cotton fabrics: wine red and dark green, 87cm by 152cm each; yellow, 88cm by 26cm; green, 88cm by 33cm; white, 88cm by 18cm; pink, 64cm by 16cm; orange, 90cm by 18cm; blue, 72cm by 32cm; navy blue, 90cm by 53cm; red, 90cm by 21cm; purple, 90cm by 23cm; cobalt blue, 88cm by 23cm; beige, 88cm by 240cm. 8 button moulds, 3.5cm in diameter and 4 button moulds, 1.8cm in diameter.

FINISHED SIZE: 147cm square

DIRECTIONS:

1. Cut out pieces for Front, adding 1cm seam allowance all around.
2. Sew pieces of center square together in same manner as Cushion Cover. Sew pieces of each block together and then assemble blocks.
3. Cover button moulds with indicated fabrics and sew them in place.
4. Cut out Back pieces and sew them together.
5. Place pieced Front on Back with wrong sides together. Turn margin of Back over edges of Front. Turn in 1cm of margin and slip-stitch edging to Front.

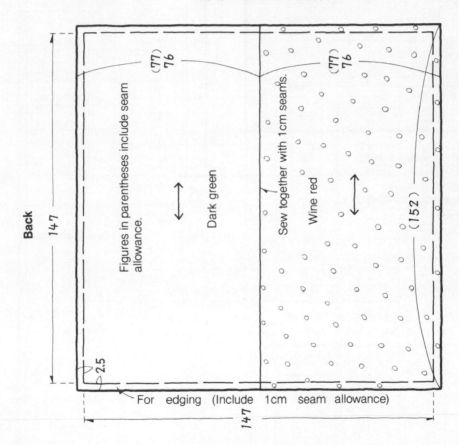

Back

147

2.5

Figures in parentheses include seam allowance.

Dark green

Sew together with 1cm seams.

Wine red

(77) 76

(77) 76

(152)

For edging (Include 1cm seam allowance)

147

TOTE BAGS, shown on pages 40 and 41, top

MATERIALS: Cotton fabrics (See the photo for colors and designs.): 90cm by 45cm for (a); 90cm square for (b). #50 white cotton sewing thread. One pair of bamboo handles, 13.5cm wide.
FINISHED SIZE: See the diagram.

DIRECTIONS:
1. Cut out pieces, adding seam allowance. Starting in center and working around and outward, sew pieces together, using method C on page 105. Press seams open.
2. Make up for bag, following instructions (A) through (D).

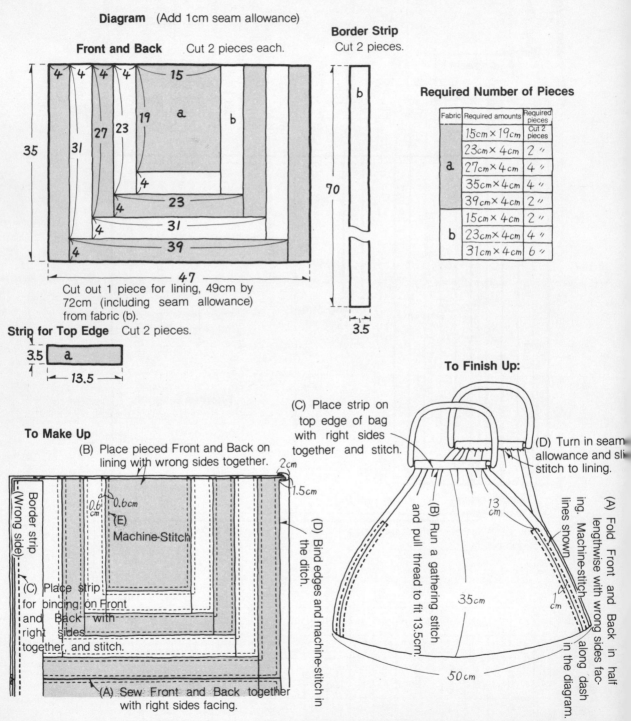

Diagram (Add 1cm seam allowance)

Front and Back Cut 2 pieces each.

Cut out 1 piece for lining, 49cm by 72cm (including seam allowance) from fabric (b).

Strip for Top Edge Cut 2 pieces.

Border Strip Cut 2 pieces.

Required Number of Pieces

Fabric	Required amounts	Required pieces
a	15cm × 19cm	Cut 2 pieces
	23cm × 4cm	2 ″
	27cm × 4cm	4 ″
	35cm × 4cm	4 ″
	39cm × 4cm	2 ″
b	15cm × 4cm	2 ″
	23cm × 4cm	4 ″
	31cm × 4cm	6 ″

To Make Up

(B) Place pieced Front and Back on lining with wrong sides together.

(E) Machine-Stitch

(C) Place strip for binding on Front and Back with right sides together, and stitch.

(A) Sew Front and Back together with right sides facing.

(D) Bind edges and machine-stitch in the ditch.

(C) Place strip on top edge of bag with right sides together and stitch.

To Finish Up:

(D) Turn in seam allowance and slip stitch to lining.

(A) Fold Front and Back in half lengthwise with wrong sides facing. Machine-stitch along dash lines shown in the diagram.

(B) Run a gathering stitch and pull thread to fit 13.5cm.

STRIPED PURSES, shown on pages 40 and 41, bottom

MATERIALS: Cotton fabrics (See the photo for colors and designs.): 23cm by 31cm for (c); 9cm by 31cm for (d); 7cm by 31cm for (e). #50 white cotton sewing thread. Purse frame, 11.5cm wide (gold frame for red purse and silver, for green one).

FINISHED SIZE: See the diagram.

DIRECTIONS:
1. Cut out pieces, adding seam allowance. Sew pieces together, using method C on page 105. Press seams open. Round corners as shown.
2. Place pieced top on lining with wrong sides together and machine-stitch as shown in the diagram.
3. Fold lined top in half lengthwise. Bind each side with strip. Back-stitch through punched holes in metal frame to top edges.

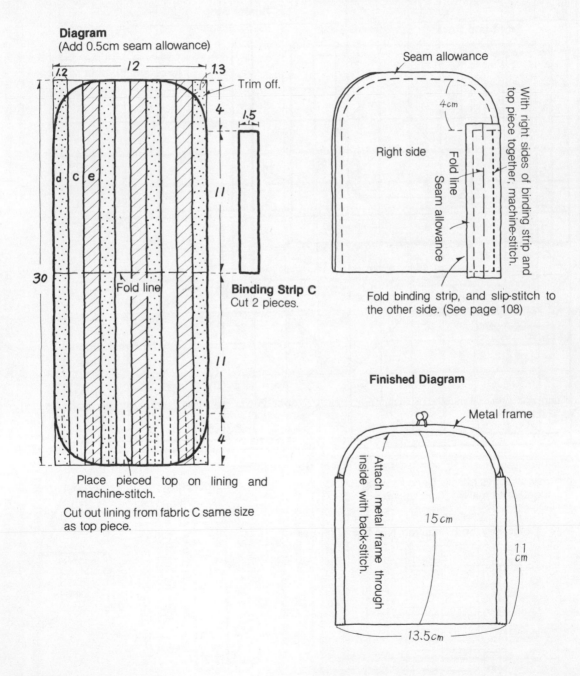

Diagram
(Add 0.5cm seam allowance)

Trim off.

d c e

Fold line

30

Place pieced top on lining and machine-stitch.

Cut out lining from fabric C same size as top piece.

Binding Strip C
Cut 2 pieces.

Seam allowance

Right side

4cm

Fold line
Seam allowance

With right sides of binding strip and top piece together, machine-stitch.

Fold binding strip, and slip-stitch to the other side. (See page 108)

Finished Diagram

Metal frame

Attach metal frame through inside with back-stitch.

15 cm

11 cm

13.5 cm

TABLECLOTH, shown on pages 20 and 21

Diagram

Front   (Add 0.7cm seam allowance)

Half-back stitch with black thread 0.1cm in from seams showing very little stitches.

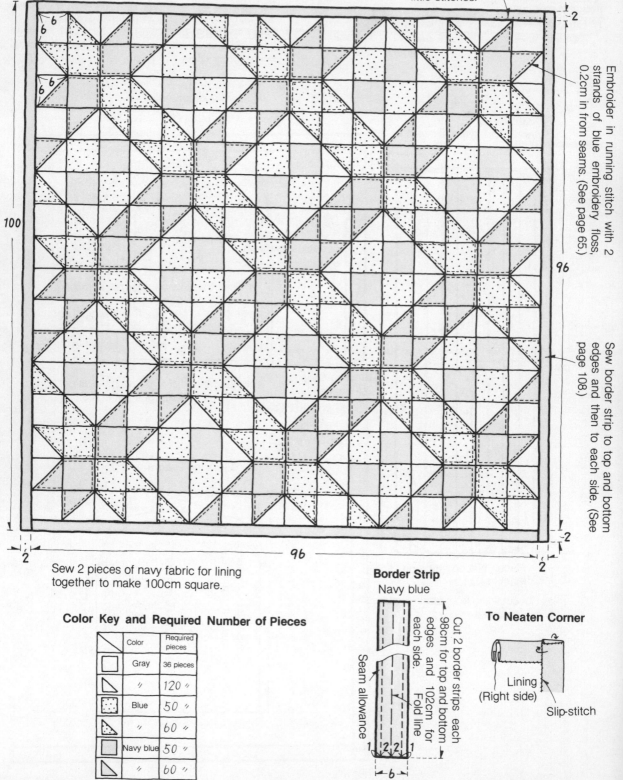

Embroider in running stitch with 2 strands of blue embroidery floss, 0.2cm in from seams. (See page 65.)

Sew border strip to top and bottom edges and then to each side. (See page 108.)

100

96

96

2

2

2

2

6
6

6
6

Sew 2 pieces of navy fabric for lining together to make 100cm square.

Border Strip

Navy blue

Cut 2 border strips each 98cm for top and bottom edges and 102cm for each side.

Fold line

Seam allowance

1 2 2 1

6

To Neaten Corner

Lining (Right side)

Slip-stitch

Color Key and Required Number of Pieces

	Color	Required pieces
	Gray	36 pieces
	″	120 ″
	Blue	50 ″
	″	60 ″
	Navy blue	50 ″
	″	60 ″

MATERIALS: Cotton fabrics: gray, 114cm by 171cm; navy blue, 90cm by 120cm; blue, 90cm by 100cm; lightweight cotton fabric in navy blue for lining, 51cm by 200cm. #25 six-strand embroidery floss in blue. #20 heavy-duty black cotton sewing thread.

FINISHED SIZE: 100cm square (Underlay, 118cm square)

DIRECTIONS:

1. Cut out pieces, adding seam allowance. Sew pieces together, using method C on page 105. Press seams open.

2. Embroider in running stitch with blue embroidery floss along dash lines shown in the diagram.

3. Cut out strips for border. With right sides together, sew strips to edges of pieced top. Turn to right side. Half-back stitch along edges of border showing very little stitches.

4. Cut out pieces for border of underlay. Sew 17 pieces together for each side and 19 pieces each for top and bottom. Sew pieced strips to top and bottom of gray fabric, and then to each side.

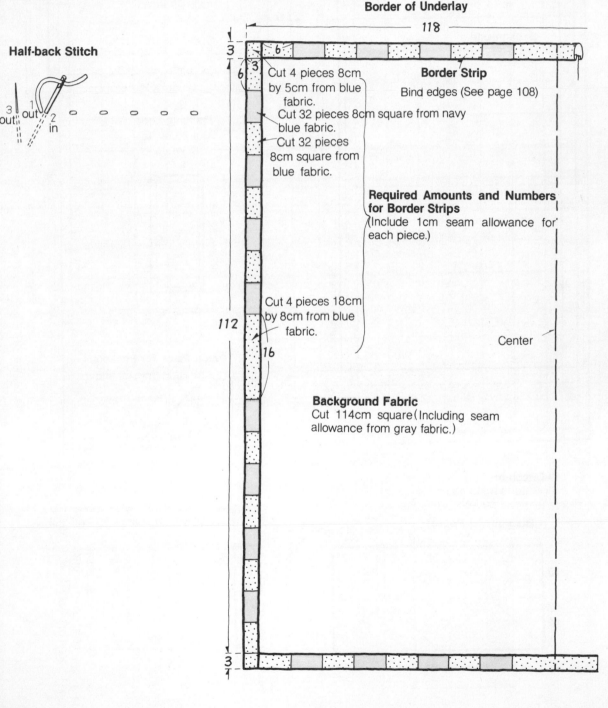

Half-back Stitch

Border of Underlay

118

3

6   3

6

Border Strip

Cut 4 pieces 8cm by 5cm from blue fabric.

Bind edges (See page 108)

Cut 32 pieces 8cm square from navy blue fabric.

Cut 32 pieces 8cm square from blue fabric.

Required Amounts and Numbers for Border Strips
(Include 1cm seam allowance for each piece.)

Cut 4 pieces 18cm by 8cm from blue fabric.

112

16

Center

Background Fabric
Cut 114cm square (Including seam allowance from gray fabric.)

3

POCKETED WALL HANGING, shown on page 42

MATERIALS: Cotton fabrics (See the photo for colors and designs.): 90cm by 68cm for (a); 90cm by 103cm for (b). #50 white cotton sewing thread.

FINISHED SIZE: See the diagram.

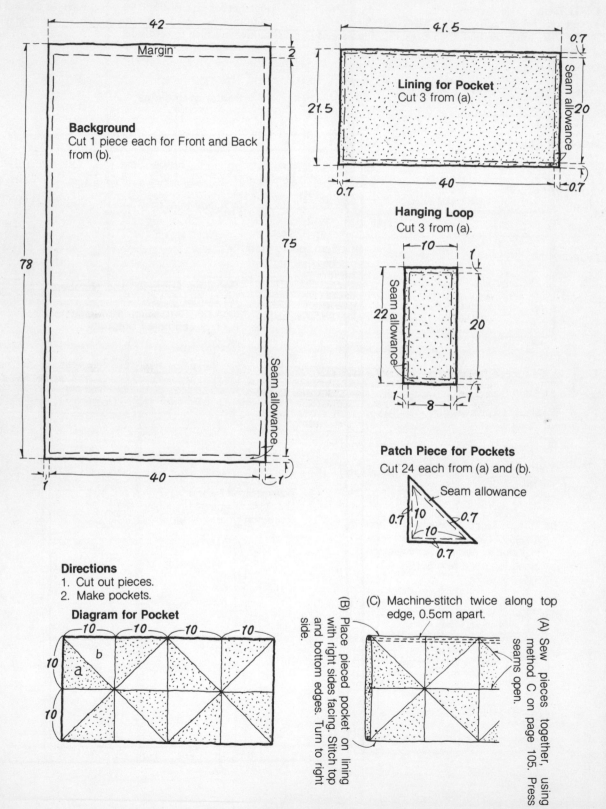

Background
Cut 1 piece each for Front and Back from (b).

42

Margin

2

78

75

Seam allowance

40

1

1

41.5

0.7

Lining for Pocket
Cut 3 from (a).

21.5

20

Seam allowance

0.7

40

0.7

Hanging Loop
Cut 3 from (a).

10

1

22

Seam allowance

20

1

8

1

Patch Piece for Pockets
Cut 24 each from (a) and (b).

Seam allowance

0.7   10   0.7

10

0.7

Directions
1. Cut out pieces.
2. Make pockets.

Diagram for Pocket

10   10   10   10

10   b   a

10

(C) Machine-stitch twice along top edge, 0.5cm apart.

(B) Place pieced pocket on lining with right sides facing. Stitch top and bottom edges. Turn to right side.

(A) Sew pieces together, using method C on page 105. Press seams open.

90

3. Place pockets on background. Machine-stitch along bottom edge of each pocket.

4. Place Front of background on Back with right sides together. Stitch three sides, leaving top open. Turn to right side.

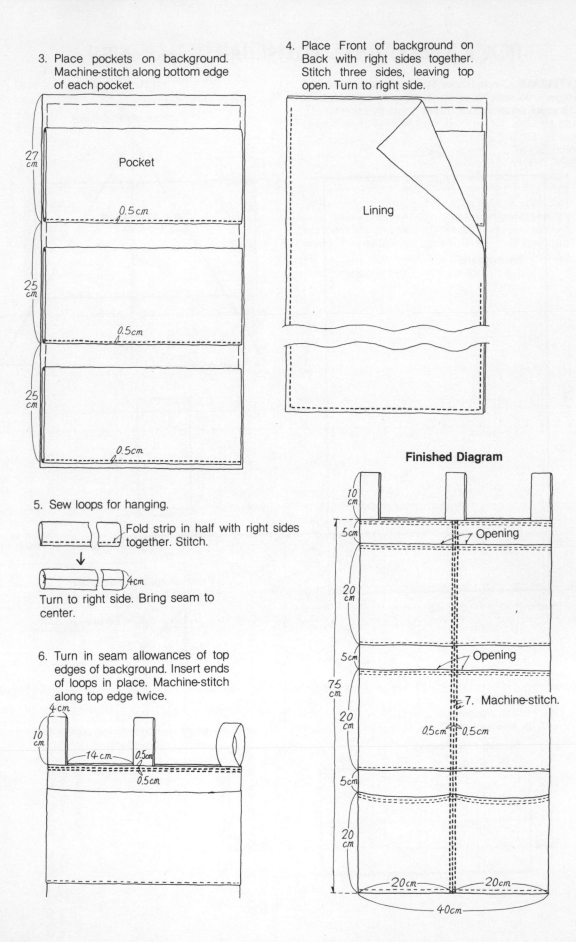

27 cm

Pocket

0.5 cm

25 cm

0.5 cm

25 cm

0.5 cm

Lining

Finished Diagram

10 cm

5 cm

Opening

20 cm

5 cm

Opening

75 cm

7. Machine-stitch.

20 cm

0.5 cm   0.5 cm

5 cm

20 cm

20 cm   20 cm

40 cm

5. Sew loops for hanging.

Fold strip in half with right sides together. Stitch.

↓

4 cm

Turn to right side. Bring seam to center.

6. Turn in seam allowances of top edges of background. Insert ends of loops in place. Machine-stitch along top edge twice.

4 cm

10 cm

14 cm   0.5 cm

0.5 cm

THOUSAND PYRAMIDS TABLE RUNNER,

shown on pages 46 and 47

MATERIALS: Cotton fabrics (See the photo for colors and designs.): 90cm by 100cm for (a); 90cm by 17cm each for (b) and (f); 90cm by 35cm for (c); 90cm by 43cm for (d); 90cm by 26cm for (e); pink with white dots for lining, 58cm by 134cm.

FINISHED SIZE: 58cm by 134cm

DIRECTIONS:

1. Make templates. Cut out pieces, adding seam allowance.
2. Following the diagram, sew pieces together, using method A on page 102.
3. Cut out strips from fabric (a) on the bias and sew them together. Place pieced patches on lining with wrong sides facing. Bind edges with bias-cut strip.

Pattern (Actual Size)

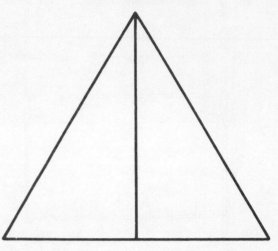

Diagram

Front

(Add 0.7cm seam allowance all around. Place patch pieces symmetrically.)

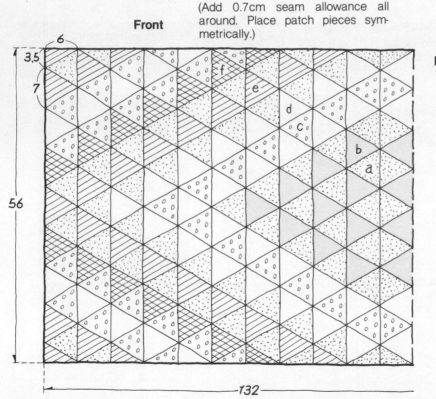

Required Number of Patch Pieces

	△	◺	◿
a	102 pieces	8 pieces	8 pieces
b	28 pieces		
c	62 pieces	4 pieces	4 pieces
d	76 pieces	2 pieces	2 pieces
e	38 pieces	6 pieces	6 pieces
f	24 pieces	2 pieces	2 pieces

Finished Diagram

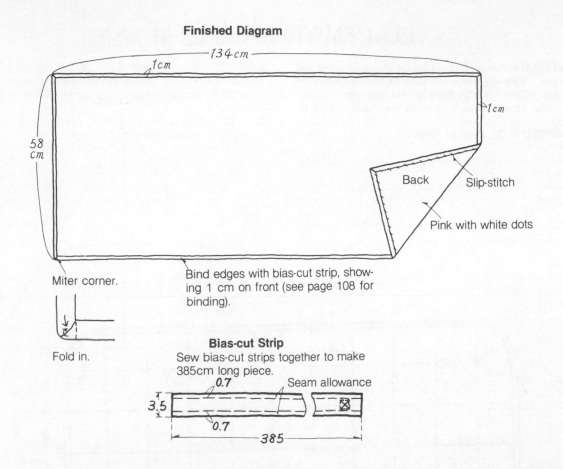

134 cm

1 cm

1 cm

58 cm

Back

Slip-stitch

Pink with white dots

Miter corner.

Fold in.

Bind edges with bias-cut strip, showing 1 cm on front (see page 108 for binding).

Bias-cut Strip

Sew bias-cut strips together to make 385cm long piece.

3.5

0.7

0.7

Seam allowance

385

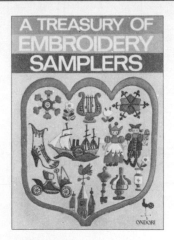

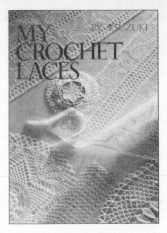

PLACEMAT, shown on page 48

MATERIALS: Cotton fabrics (See the photo for colors and designs.): 5cm square for (a); 20cm by 5cm for (b); 60cm by 5cm for (c); 69cm by 36cm for (d); 90cm by 15cm for (e). Bias tape in matching color with (d), 1.2cm by 160cm.

FINISHED SIZE: 44cm by 36cm

DIRECTIONS:
1. Cut out pieces, adding 0.5cm seam allowance all around. Sew pieces together, using method A on page 102.
2. With wrong sides of pieced patches and lining together, bind edges with bias tape.

Diagram

a = Cut 1 piece.   d = Cut 32 pieces.
b = Cut 4 pieces.   e = Cut 50 pieces.
c = Cut 12 pieces.

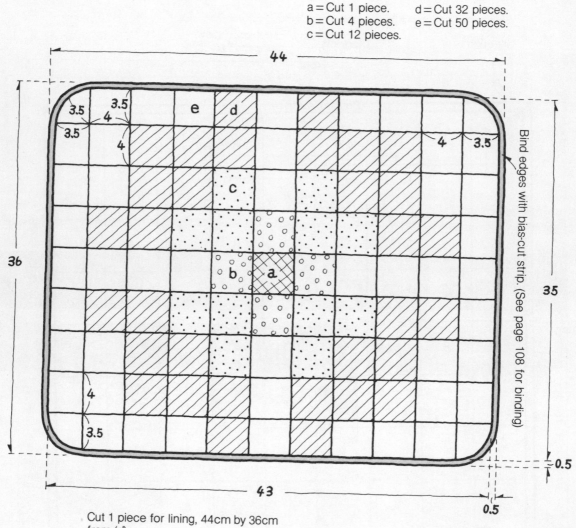

Cut 1 piece for lining, 44cm by 36cm from (d).

BOX QUILT COVERLET, shown on pages 44 and 45

MATERIALS: Cotton fabrics (See the photo for colors and designs.): 90cm by 15cm for (a); 84cm by 28cm for (b); 90cm by 112cm for (c); 90cm by 60cm each for (d) and (d'); 85cm by 51cm each for (e) (f) and (g); 20cm by 143cm for (h); wine red with small flowers for lining, 71.5cm by 282cm. #25 six-strand embroidery floss in colors to match fabrics (e) (f) and (g). Quilt batting, 140cm square.

FINISHED SIZE: 140cm square

DIRECTIONS:
1. Cut out pieces for (A) and (B) blocks, adding seam allowance. Sew pieces together, using method A on page 102.
2. Cut out pieces for (e) (f) and (g), adding seam allowance. Transfer quilting pattern to each piece of (e) (f) and (g).
3. Sew blocks (A) (B) (e) (f) and (g) together, following the diagram. Place pieced top on batting and baste. Quilt on blocks (e) (f) and (g).
4. Sew borders as shown.

Diagram

Front (Add 1cm seam allowance)

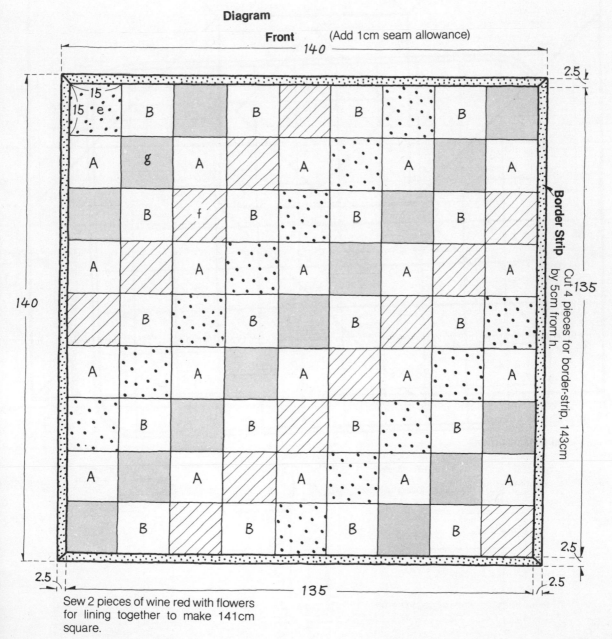

Sew 2 pieces of wine red with flowers for lining together to make 141cm square.

95

Patterns (Actual Size)   (Add 1cm seam allowance)

Patterns for (A) and (B) Blocks.
Cut 20 pieces each for (A) and (B).
Reverse the pattern for(B) block.

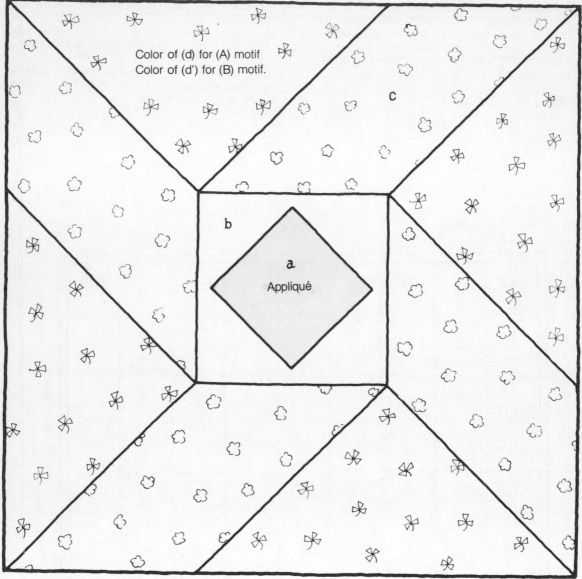

Color of (d) for (A) motif
Color of (d') for (B) motif.

c

b

a
Appliqué

Color of (d') is same as (d), but has
light pink flowers.

To Miter Corner:
1. Place strip for border on edge of
    pieced top, with right sides
    together and stitch.

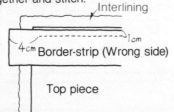

Interlining

1cm

4cm Border-strip (Wrong side)

Top piece

(Sew strips to other edges in same
manner.)

2. Sew ends of strips diagonally,
    matching the corner.

3. Turn to right side.

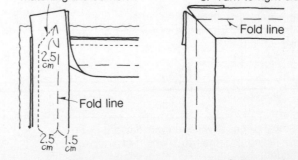

Fold line

2.5 cm

Fold line

2.5 cm   1.5 cm

Pattern (Actual Size)

(Add 1cm seam allowance)
Cut 13 pieces each for (e) and (f).
Cut 15 pieces for (g).

Quilting Pattern for (e) (f) and (g)

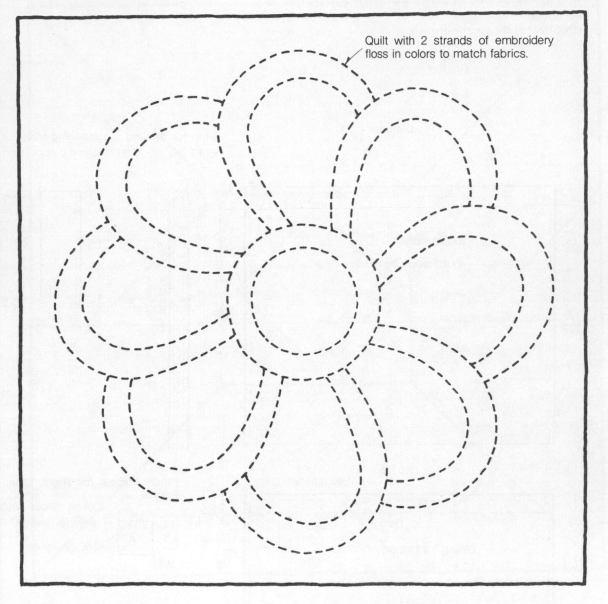

Quilt with 2 strands of embroidery floss in colors to match fabrics.

4. Turn excess to back.
   Turn in seam allowance of lining and slip-stitch.

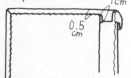

1cm
0.5 cm

POCKETED WALL HANGING, shown on page 43

MATERIALS: Cotton fabrics (See the photo for colors and designs.): 90cm by 102cm for (c); 62cm by 53cm for (d); 90cm by 20cm each for (e) and (f). #50 white cotton sewing thread.

FINISHED SIZE: See the diagram.

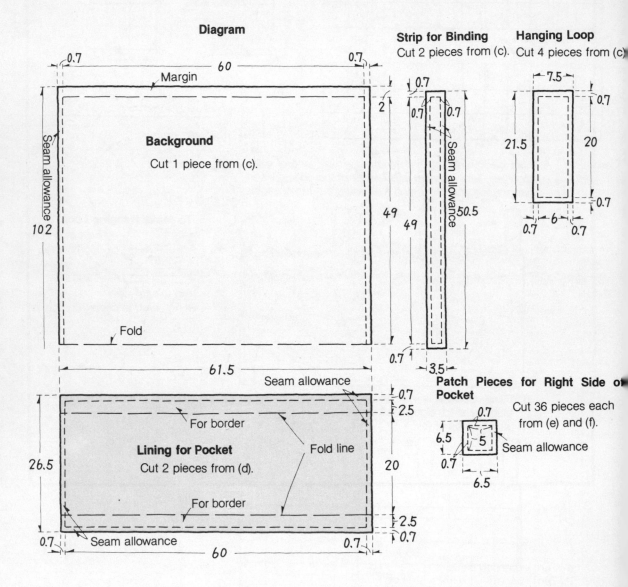

Diagram

Margin

Background

Cut 1 piece from (c).

Seam allowance

102

60

0.7

0.7

49

Fold

61.5

Seam allowance

For border

Lining for Pocket

Cut 2 pieces from (d).

Fold line

For border

26.5

0.7

Seam allowance

0.7

60

0.7

Strip for Binding
Cut 2 pieces from (c).

0.7

0.7 0.7

2

Seam allowance

50.5

49

0.7

3.5

0.7

2.5

20

2.5

0.7

Hanging Loop
Cut 4 pieces from (c)

7.5

0.7

21.5

20

0.7

0.7 6 0.7

Patch Pieces for Right Side of Pocket

Cut 36 pieces each from (e) and (f).

0.7

6.5

5

Seam allowance

0.7

6.5

Directions

1. Cut out pieces, adding seam allowance.
2. Sew pieces for pockets together, using method C on page 105. Press seams open.

Pocket (1)

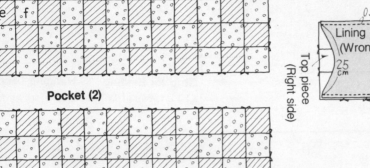

Pocket (2)

3. Place pieced pocket on lining with right sides facing. Stitch top and bottom edges.

4 Turn to right side. Crease lining 2.5cm from seams at top and bottom. Machine-stitch in the ditch of the top seam.

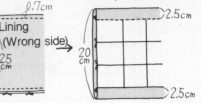

5. Fold background in half lengthwise with wrong sides together. Turn in seam allowances of top edges. Insert hanging loops in place and machine-stitch along edges.

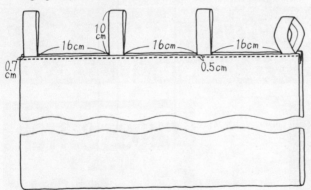

To Make Hanging Loop

Fold strip in half lengthwise with right sides together and stitch.

Turn to right side.
Bring seam to center and press.

6. Place pockets on background. Machine-stitch along dash lines of (a), and then of (b).

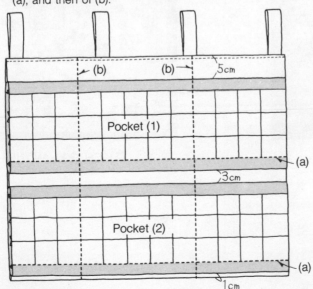

(Finished Diagram is on next page.)

Finished Diagram

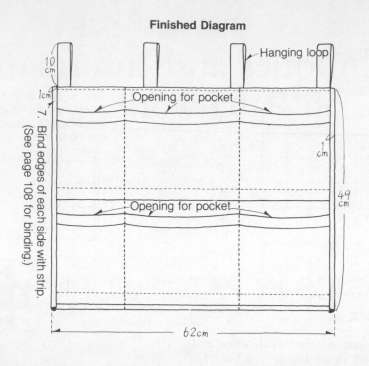

Hanging loop

10 cm

1cm

7. Bind edges of each side with strip. (See page 108 for binding.)

Opening for pocket

1 cm

49 cm

Opening for pocket

62cm

Basic Techniques and Informations on Patchwork

BASICS IN PATCHWORK

FABRIC: To make a piece of patchwork, many small patches are sewn together. Therefore, too thick, too thin, or easy to fray fabrics are not suitable to use for patchwork. Medium-weight plain-weave cotton fabrics are considered to be easily handled. Wash the fabric for pre-shrinking and removal of starch when you use new one. Press before you use.

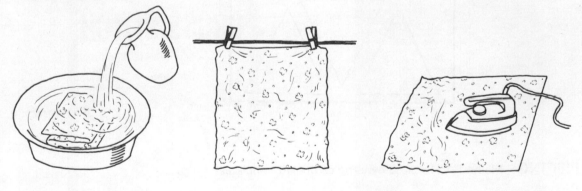

THREAD: To piece by hand: Use cotton sewing thread or mercerized No. 30 — 50 cotton thread. (If cotton thread in colors to match fabrics is not available, silk sewing thread or embroidery floss can be replaced.) To piece by machine: Use any thread to match fabrics and to be used by machine.

Cotton thread

Silk sewing thread

Embroidery thread

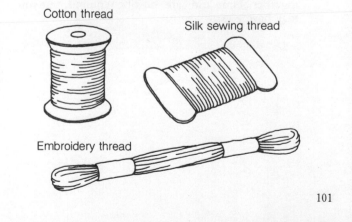

CUTTING: 1. Make actual-size patterns with cardboard or plastic sheet.

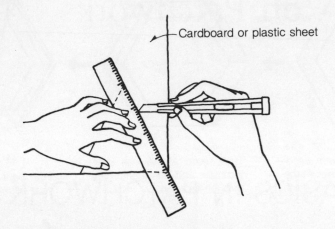

Cardboard or plastic sheet

2. Place cardboard patterns on wrong side of fabric and trace around each pattern accurately, leaving space between patterns twice as wide as seam allowance (about 1cm — 2cm).
(To cut pieces accurately is a must for a neater finish.)

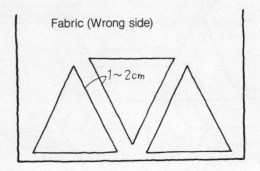

Fabric (Wrong side)

1~2cm

PIECING: Method A (To piece by using cardboard templates)

This is the most traditional method to sew pieces together. Time and care must be required, but you may have a neater finish.

102

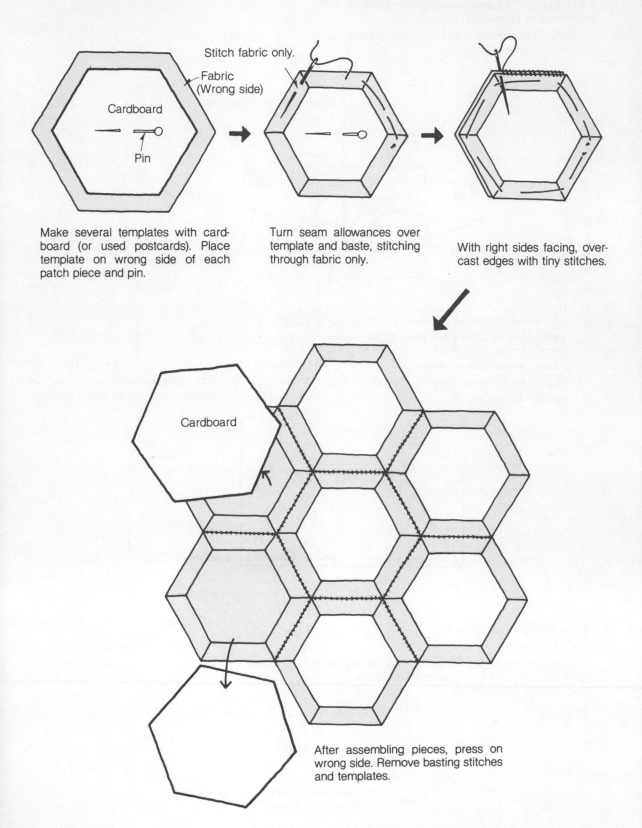

Stitch fabric only.

Fabric
(Wrong side)

Cardboard

Pin

Make several templates with cardboard (or used postcards). Place
template on wrong side of each
patch piece and pin.

Turn seam allowances over
template and baste, stitching
through fabric only.

With right sides facing, overcast edges with tiny stitches.

Cardboard

After assembling pieces, press on
wrong side. Remove basting stitches
and templates.

Method B (To piece by hand)

This is the easiest method to piece straight seams.
Turn seams to one side.

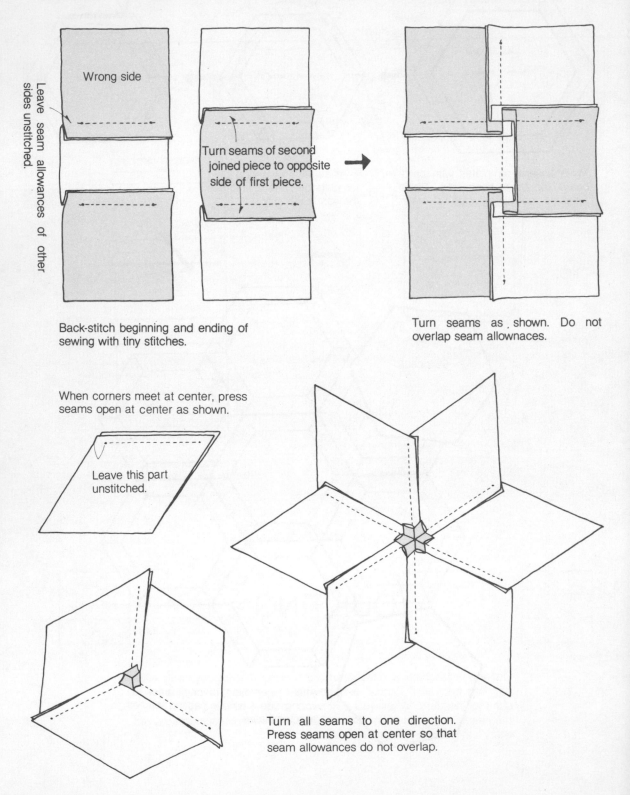

Leave seam allowances of other sides unstitched.

Wrong side

Turn seams of second joined piece to opposite side of first piece.

Back-stitch beginning and ending of sewing with tiny stitches.

Turn seams as shown. Do not overlap seam allownaces.

When corners meet at center, press seams open at center as shown.

Leave this part unstitched.

Turn all seams to one direction. Press seams open at center so that seam allowances do not overlap.

Method C (To piece by machine)

Piecing by machine is time-saving, when you are making a big project. Seams are usually pressed open, but sometimes turned to one side.

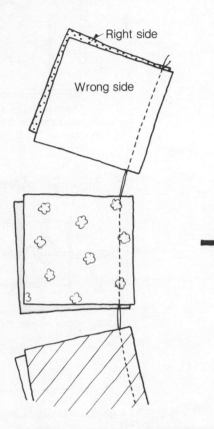

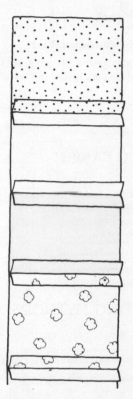

Sew one pair of pieces together by machine and continue to sew pairs of pieces without cutting thread.

Cut thread between pairs and then sew pairs of pieces together.

QUILTING

Quilting is stitching two layers of top piece and lining together with padding between. Cotton and polyester quilt batting or flannel is used for padding. When you quilt by hand using running stitch, push the needle down through all the thicknesses, then push it up again at every stitch for a neater finish.

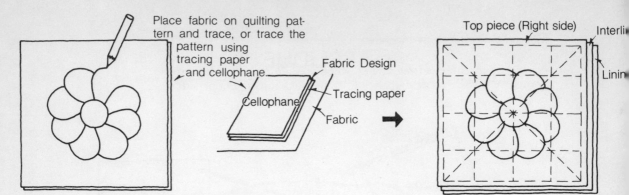

Place fabric on quilting pattern and trace, or trace the pattern using tracing paper and cellophane.

Fabric Design
Tracing paper
Cellophane
Fabric

Top piece (Right side)
Interli
Linin

Transfer quilting patterns to right side of top pieces, except pieces to be quilted along seams.
Draw straight lines directly on right side of top pieces with help of ruler.

Place quilt top, batting and lining together and baste three layers. Quilt along quilting lines.

LINING FABRIC

Soft-finish cotton fabric of loose weave as sheeting canmore easily quilted than closely-woven cotton broadcloth.

Movement of Needle

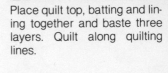

Thread
Fabric
Needle
1 stitch

Push needle down vertically.

QUILTING METHODS:

Quilt on seams (stitch in the ditch).   Quilt along seams.   Quilt diagonally in two directions.

 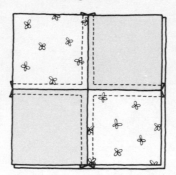 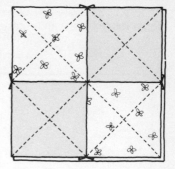

Quilt along quilting design.

APPLIQUE

Slip-stitch

Seam allowance

Slip-stitch vertically, showing very little stitches.
(Turn in seam allowance at curves with help of needle as you sew.)

MAKING BIAS TAPE

CUTTING
Cut strips on the bias.

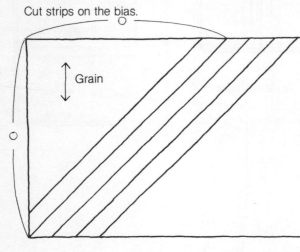

Grain

PIECING
Join ends of strips.

Right side

Wrong side

Press seams open.

Wrong side

BOUND EDGE

To Bind Edge

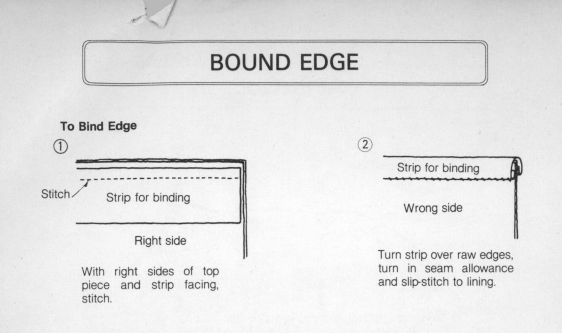

① Stitch

Strip for binding

Right side

With right sides of top piece and strip facing, stitch.

② Strip for binding

Wrong side

Turn strip over raw edges, turn in seam allowance and slip-stitch to lining.

SEWING INSTRUCTIONS FOR PILLOW

Make opening with zipper on the back, two thirds away from the edge, so that you can easily slip on and off for washing. Make inner pillow 1cm larger than the size of outer pillow. Tear kapok off into small pieces and stuff into inner pillow. Slip-stitch opening closed with tiny stitches.

Sewing Diagram for Outer Pillow

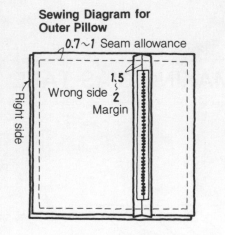

0.7~1 Seam allowance

Right side

Wrong side

1.5 ~ 2 Margin

Sewing Diagram for Inner Pillow

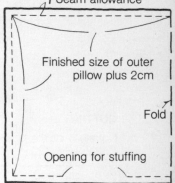

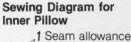

1 Seam allowance

Finished size of outer pillow plus 2cm

Fold

Opening for stuffing

To Sew Zipper

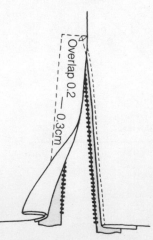

Overlap 0.2

0.3cm